"Unwanted is the story of a woman who grew up neglected and abused but became the activist-mother of a Down syndrome son and a fundraiser who raised half a billion dollars for charity. There is no one in this world like Linda Smith."

—**The Honorable Oscar Goodman,** Las Vegas Mayor.

"A powerful and searingly honest memoir that tells the story of one woman's journey from homelessness and neglect to Las Vegas fundraising icon. For those who have struggled to make sense of a life filled with seemingly insurmountable obstacles. . .this book will give you the courage to charge forward with resolve."

—**Jan Laverty Jones,** Caesars Entertainment.

"Eleanor Roosevelt said, 'No one can make you feel inferior without your consent.' When Linda Smith was told her son was inferior, she fought back. Her life story is a must-read account of how a mother's love and courage secured her son's right to live and flourish, and championed the rights of every child fighting the label of 'disabled.'

—**Tom Thomas,** Thomas and Mack Co.

"What Linda has done for those with intellectual disabilities is astonishing. I'm not a religious man, but this woman should be sainted."

—**Penn Jillette** of Penn & Teller

"This must-read book is the story of an amazing woman and family."

—**Rob Goldstein,** President and COO, Las Vegas Sands Hotel.

"Linda's book brings to light a terrible secret in the world of disability rights; freedom, the right to live, and sometimes. . .just to exist."

—**Molly Nocum,** CEO, Noah Homes

"This is an intimate account of a mother's journey to right the wrongs. It is raw, painful, funny and exhilarating."

—**Bill Walters,** Professional Gambler

"With a 'take no prisoner,' 'no is not an option' approach to life, Linda's tome; Unwanted, takes us on a roller coaster journey, teaching lessons of life and love and the inestimable worth of every person."

—**Charmaine Solomon President,** My Possibilities Texas.

"Linda Smith's memoir, Unwanted, is an inspiring account of a mother's mission to give her profoundly disabled son's life meaning, and the amazing personal growth and community support she created as she discovered her own potential."

—**Scott Nielson,** Chairman of the Opportunity Village
Foundation Board

"Linda Smith's book is filled with adventure, hardships, romance, overwhelming challenges, and undeniable love. Linda captures and expresses each scene as only she can. I hope, like me, you enjoy, appreciate, learn, and marvel at the life you're about to read."

—**Bobby Bigelow**

"Thank you, Linda, for sharing your amazing story as a fiercely compassionate woman and mother. You have demanded and blazed a path of support for your son and changed the lives of thousands more along the way."

—**Patty Mitchell & Susan Dlouhy,** Passion Works Studio &
Creative Abundance Consulting

"You don't have to have a Down syndrome child or an immigration problem to be profoundly touched by this book. Unwanted is about triumph over adversity. You will cry, laugh, feel empowered, and hopefully find joy, even when life throws you a curve ball"

—**Marsala Rypka,** Celebrity Scribe
and Co-Founder of The CLASS Project.

LINDA SMITH

U̶NWANTED

HOW A MOTHER LEARNED TO TURN SHAME, GRIEF AND FEAR INTO PURPOSE, PASSION AND EMPOWERMENT

Cover and interior design: Nord Compo

ISBN 978-0-9992276-1-9 (hard cover)
ISBN 978-0-9992276-0-2 (paperback)
ISBN 978-0-9992276-3-3 (digital)

"Being unwanted, unloved, uncared for, forgotten by everybody, I think that is a much greater hunger, a much greater poverty than the person who has nothing to eat."

Mother Teresa

Dedicated to Christopher, Jason, John, Krysti and Lilyclaire.

CHAPTER ONE

THE GOOD NEWS IS. . .
HE WON'T LIVE LONG

An all-enveloping sadness permeated the room.

May 15, 1970. That was the day the earth shifted—the day an ambulance with flashing lights and sirens, raced along the tarmac at Toronto's Pearson airport to greet an inbound emergency flight from Las Vegas with a pregnant woman on board who was in labor. That was the day my six-pound son, my thief of dreams, arrived two weeks early, gasping for breath.

The decision for me to fly home to Canada so close to my due date made perfect sense at the time. My entertainer husband, Glenn, was finishing an engagement at the Flamingo Hotel with Wayne Newton in Las Vegas, were we now lived, and he was scheduled to perform in Toronto in two weeks.

Going ahead of him would give me the opportunity to line up a delivery doctor, make arrangements with the hospital, and prepare for the birth. My mother and sister had a home in Toronto.

On the ride to the hospital, I silently prayed. *Please God, let everything be okay.*

An hour later, my baby boy entered the world. Considering the riotous events of the past eight hours, the room was eerily quiet. The lights were dim, but I could see the doctor's face as he pursed his lips and frowned, then raised his brow and nodded wordless instructions to the nurse to take the baby.

I felt the blood drain from my face, and I began to shiver uncontrollably, afraid of the words that might tumble from my cold lips. *Is he stillborn? Is everything okay?* And then I heard it—a weak cry emanating from my naked baby as the nurse glanced my way with an equally weak smile. Before she whisked the tiny bundle away, I noted with relief the correct number of arms, legs, fingers, and toes.

It remained quiet in the room as the medical team went about their business. It had been an eventful labor and delivery, and I felt myself on the verge of tears.

C'mon Linda, you made it; the worst is over.

I could see the eyes of the emergency room doctor through my splayed legs. He did not look at me as he calmly went about his business. I tried to make eye contact, but he was not interested. With determined preoccupation, he finished tying up the loose ends of an emergency delivery. "Do you have family nearby?" he asked softly.

I shook my head no as I shivered uncontrollably, I had endured several hours of excruciating labor and off-the-charts contractions midair at 35,000 feet with no idea when it might end, only to end up in a strange hospital, alone and screaming for help in the labor room, where all I received was a frown from the doctor and the nurse.

I was pale and in shock when the doctor quietly and matter-of-factly stated that I had just had a baby boy.

The entire birth experience had been brutal, something I never wanted to do it again. I expected smiles and good wishes, but there were none, not from the doctor or any of the nurses in the delivery room.

For some reason an all-enveloping sadness permeated the air.

After giving birth I called Glenn in Las Vegas, and even though I was exhausted from the ordeal, I reveled in telling him what happened on the flight, the long, hard labor, and the birth of our beautiful, perfect little boy whom I had yet to officially meet because the hospital staff was running some routine tests.

Then Glenn passed the phone to Wayne Newton, Fats Domino, the band members, a few cocktail waitresses, a couple of bartender pals, and finally my hooker friend. Everyone was excited and loved hearing the details of the in-flight labor. Soon a big bouquet of flowers arrived, and I smiled as I drifted off to sleep.

When I awoke a short time later, I heard babies crying, people celebrating, and footsteps coming and going outside my room. I had just asked a young candy striper to find a nurse who could tell me when I would see my baby when a contingent of white-clad medical staff arrived and stood in stony silence at the foot of the bed as far from me as decorum would permit. I noticed how stiff and uncomfortable the delivery doctor and the others looked and I thought that was strange on such a happy occasion.

"Do you understand the meaning of chromosome abnormalities?" he began.

HUH? I stared at him blankly.

"I am sorry to tell you this, but your baby was born severely disabled. We knew right away that he has multiple problems based on certain obvious characteristics, but we had to run tests to confirm our suspicions."

The doctor paused as I stared at him not comprehending what he was saying.

"Unfortunately, he is the first baby born with a disability in our newly-renovated delivery room. We have all been involved in the protocols for such births, which is why we did not tell you right away...that and the fact that your husband or other family members were not here to assist with the bad news."

What?

"We checked your chromosomes, and there is nothing wrong with you. These things just happen; it's a fluke, a freak of nature."

Freak? Oh God, please stop them from uttering these words. Make them go away.

"The good news is. . .he won't live long." This was stated in a more upbeat tone.

I closed my eyes and waited.

Surely this is a dream? My son is not going to die. I saw him; he is perfect. Did they swap my beautiful baby with another one?

"Your son has a heart defect and respiratory problems, typical for children with his condition. He has Down syndrome, more commonly referred to as Mongolism and mental retardation. He is very ill and not expected to survive. This is a blessing. You should forget about him and concentrate on having another baby."

And then.

"Is there anyone we can call?"

I did not utter a word. I was the dark cloud in their day, and they fled the room after relieving themselves of the wretched news.

My son was one day old, and already he had been rejected. I didn't know it then, but he would face a lifetime of rejections. And I would spend my life fighting for him, seeking a place in the world where he would be welcome. To do so, I would have to draw on the lessons I learned during my own painful, and often terrifying childhood.

CHAPTER TWO

THE HOUSE BLEW UP

We kids were nonexistent to them, born into dysfunction and left to fend for ourselves.

I was only six years old when it happened, but I remember the day my father blew up our house. It was a cold and drizzly British Saturday morning. Boom, boom, boom! I heard and felt the explosion as the blue and orange fire shot across the kitchen from the fireplace and knocked me to the floor. My ears rang as I lay on my back, eyes wide, taking in the purple, red, and yellow colors. Boom, boom, boom again. I was a silent witness, fascinated by the awesomeness of the explosions and the shudder and shriek of the house as it wobbled on its foundation. I smelled the gasoline, the fire, and my singed hair. In the distance, I heard a door slam, and I saw my father, a blur through the smoke, run out the back.

Hey. . .I'm here.

Dazed, I tried to get up. The screeching, unintelligible sounds in the small confines of the room were deafening.

"Get out."

A large hand reached out and dragged me, dazed and disoriented, toward the front door, then out onto the porch.

Next I heard loud noises; angry, aggressive voices; feet running; screams of terror; and filthy words. The smell and taste of smoke and gasoline seared my throat.

The home next door to ours was attached at the kitchen, and it was from this place that my rescuer, the neighbor, yelled obscenities as my father fled our smoke-filled home. My father's hands and face were blackened from the soot.

"Who knew that would happen? I was soaking my pants in petrol, and they must have ignited with the fireplace. Lil's not going to like cleaning up this mess," my father said, his words fading as he walked down the block to the bar.

I was left with the neighbor, who patted my hair saying it would grow back. This was just another white-hot, dangerous mess of a day with my father.

I was the middle child; a mouse with freckled skin, mousy hair, mousy personality, and mousy clothes - a cipher in a frightening world. My mother was beautiful, a knockout they say. A British-trained, gold medal ballroom dancer, she often performed at the Blackpool Tower. Not only talented, but creative, she designed costumes for her dance partners and friends.

My father was a normal functioning man when he went off to war. But after serving overseas for four years, he returned home a hollowed out, bitter, frustrated man, whose anger was always simmering just below the surface.

He had left his beautiful wife at home while he assisted in the war effort, and he was convinced that with the hundreds of thousands of American and Canadian GIs stationed in the UK, she had been unfaithful.

My father was bigger than life. A handsomely rakish man, he openly attracted the advances of the neighborhood wives and enjoyed the fist fights that followed.

My parents were combustible, like fire and petrol. Why they stayed together is a mystery. We kids were nonexistent to them, born into dysfunction and left to fend for ourselves. We looked out for each other. There was Jean, the brave boss of the trio; Terry, the innocent tagalong; and me, an invisible nobody, who silently watched the calamities unfold.

We lived in fear; fear of the rage, the volatile language, the physical altercations, and being embarrassed. Neighbors whispered when we passed by, protecting their children from the loathsome trio down the street.

When I was eight years old, I experienced my first love interest. Danny was the prettiest boy I ever met with lovely blond hair and the bluest of eyes. I lived across the street from him, and during my unhappy childhood years, he was the one person who was kind to me. We were inseparable. Our favorite pastime was stealing candy from the local store, running as fast as we could to avoid capture, and then delighting in the rare treat.

We would walk miles in every direction, jumping over hedges, scattering chickens, stealing an egg or a stalk of rhubarb, then sprinting away, overjoyed with our newly acquired treasure. Sharing a soda was something very special.

We had names for each other. I was "Miss Olive" and he was "Oh, Danny Boy." I didn't think it was unusual that Danny's vocabulary was limited, or that he would run to greet me with arms flapping wildly, calling out "piggy, piggy, piggy," a term of endearment that caused the neighborhood children to run in the opposite direction. There was strength in numbers, and we stuck up for each other.

~~UN~~WANTED

It wasn't until much later that I realized Danny had an intellectual disability. But he loved me without reservation, and I loved him. Danny was my first contact with the kind of unconditional love disabled people give—a kind of love I would find myself encircled in as an adult. The world we made together was kinder and gentler than any other I knew, a respite from the violence that tore my family to pieces.

CHAPTER \ THREE

FAMILY LIFE

I was ashamed of our family.

The word on the street was to stay away from our family. My father was known to raise his fists at the slightest provocation. If an unfortunate fella snuck a peek at his wife, it was reason for a knock-down, drag-out brawl.

Although it would be some time before we found out, my father used Jean as his personal battering ram, more so when she began to attract the attention of boys. He considered her his personal property. He was abusive to me, too, but that came later.

My father was musically talented and the life of the party when in the company of others. He could play instruments, sing, and make people laugh. But over the years our family lost many friendships due to his hair-trigger temper that made people uncomfortable to be around him.

I was ashamed of our family.

Stanley Park, which was only steps from our house, was where I escaped each day, where I felt at home. I would run to the park and spend hundreds of hours in this beautiful place, lying on the grassy hill away from curious eyes, imagining myself a princess in my own private garden.

There was a time when a little girl from our neighborhood went missing. A large search party was organized in a futile attempt to find her. I knew the park inside and out, and I remember thinking I would find her lost and asleep in one of my secret places. I would be the one to bring her home, and I would be a hero. But no matter how hard I searched, she remained lost for several months, until one day her little body was found in the woodlands. She had been molested and killed, and I secretly wondered if my father had done this terrible thing.

That was a heavy weight on my young shoulders until the perpetrator was finally found. It turned out he was a neighbor who had children of his own, and like my own father seemed friendly and outgoing. That discovery shocked the entire town, but I wasn't shocked. As my father's child, I already knew about deception.

When I was nine years old, my father gambled away our Stanley Park home in just a few hours. Disheartened and humiliated, we gathered our belongings and left what little security we had, while he took his usual seat at the corner pub, regaling the disinterested barkeeper of his near wins. Needless to say, the neighbors were glad to see us go.

My mother's mother owned a boarding home and reluctantly took us in. Losing our home was traumatic, but it wasn't the last time we would find ourselves without a roof over our heads. I was too young to fully understand how unstable our family was, and how tragic it was for my mother.

Family life

My father was an inveterate gambler, always on the losing end. He was a cheater, a womanizer, a thief, and a child abuser. Fortunately we would soon escape from him on a ship to North America, or so we thought.

CHAPTER \ FOUR

ESCAPE TO CANADA

Perhaps she knew a thief when she saw one.

I was besotted with our ship, aptly named the *Empress of Britain*. I was ten years old and dazzled by the luxurious chandeliers, plush carpeting, a movie theater, and other fabulous décor.

The Empress of Britain left Liverpool in early July on a five-day journey to Montreal. The massive ship had accommodations for 160 first-class passengers, but our family of four was amongst the many tourist-class travelers.

That first night, we went for dinner as the ship slowly made its way into open seas. The dining room was beautifully outfitted, and I was over the moon to learn I could order whatever I wanted. Pretty boys in wait-staff garb would politely call me "Miss" and serve me with a smile.

Prior to leaving, this beautiful beast of a ship had shifted gently in its berth alongside the docks, and I was distressed to find my equilibrium shifting too. That first visit to the dining room would be my last expedition out of our cabin as the minute the ship left the dock, I became violently ill with motion sickness that lasted throughout the entire voyage.

The constant *chug, chug,* creaks and groans of the ship echoed my despair as I lay on the bunk bed, exhausted from the constant retching. My only companion was a solitary fly, who I had much in common with. We were both insignificant, ugly and repulsive. To make things worse, I was the child of a bad man—and I had a terrible secret.

I recalled wanting to confide my father's abuse to a teacher who happened to look at me one day with what I thought was an inquiring kindness. Perhaps she recognized a vulnerable, wounded child in need.

Instead, she asked me what I had in my pocket and if I had taken a roll of candy off her desk. I had not. I did steal candy from the Woolworth counter on occasion with Danny, and I had eyed her candy with an unnatural longing. Perhaps she knew a thief when she saw one.

After five long days and nights, we entered the Saint Lawrence Seaway. With the ship drawing ever closer to the end of the journey and our new country, I regained my equilibrium and rejoined the other passengers. I slipped through the happy throngs to the rail and took in the most amazing sights. I was looking forward to our new life with optimism and resolve. We were home.

CHAPTER FIVE

ON THE RUN

I was mortified that we had come to Canada
to end up in a predicament like this.

Once we cleared immigration and customs, we gathered our meager belongings and boarded a train that took us to Toronto. We were in Canada now, thousands of miles from our past.

In the row across from us was a family with a young man who behaved in a peculiar way. He flapped his hands erratically in a circular motion; his unseeing eyes sparkled as he rocked back and forth to an inner rhythm; and his intermittent squeals of delight were interspersed with the clank and chug of the train, as his parents nervously looked on.

I stared in wonder. I had never witnessed such odd behavior. There was something in his countenance that was familiar. . . Was it his angelic face? Then I had a pang of recognition—*Danny. Oh Danny boy, I see you. . . I miss you.*

Arriving in Toronto, we settled into a routine, learned the ways of our new country, and tried to fit in. I could not believe the luxuries. There was instant heat in our apartment, which was so different from our home in England.

Although I was optimistic about our new life, I quickly came to dislike school, where our strange accents and British mannerisms made us the target of cruel jokes.

Our happiness in Canada was short lived when we received news that our father was also making his way to Canada. Over the past few months, we had managed to put our former life behind us, but now the weight and fear returned, as we went into hiding, moving from basement to basement. Neither Jean nor I discussed the abuse with our mother. Each of us assumed we were his only victim.

My mother's dancing skills made her a popular teacher, and she worked long hours at the Arthur Murray Dance Studio in downtown Toronto. Although there was some security in this job, moving around put a strain on all of us. We would hear of my father's whereabouts. We even caught glimpses of him occasionally, though we managed to avoid him, depending on the kindness of strangers, who sheltered us the best they could.

Homelessness is not for the faint of heart. It was hard for my mom and us three kids to stay in a shelter with addicts and other poor souls. But the Salvation Army epitomized the word charity, and they were our salvation. It is because of them that I became aware of the charitable sector, which would loom large in my future.

I recall one specific Christmas at the shelter, where a complete turkey dinner with all the trimmings had been served in a large hall to a gathering of poor families, compliments of one of the many benevolent societies. We were grateful for the meal, but still I hated being there.

On this occasion, all the kids were lined up while Santa Claus sat on stage and well-meaning helpers called out for us to come forward and receive a gift from Santa.

"Boy age five, girl age eight, boy age six, girl age eleven."

Wrapped gifts with a gender and age written on a gift tag determined who would receive that particular present. I held out as long as I could, until the only "girl age eleven" left was me.

I was mortified walking in front of so many solicitous faces to accept a gift, not for me, but for "girl age eleven." Humiliated, I clutched the wrapped box, and walked back the way I came. Then I stuffed the little box into a corner and never looked at it again.

Life took on a distressing rhythm of one month here, two months there, as we tried in vain to fit in. We scraped together enough money from odd jobs to put food on the table, and eventually saved enough for a few months' rent. We moved into a small efficiency apartment in central Toronto, and that's when he found us.

CHAPTER \ SIX

FOUND

*We knew he was capable of violence and had
the capacity to do much damage.*

One day there was a knock on the door, and there he was. We were shocked. He had such tremendous power over us that he walked in with his suitcase and announced he was staying. And stay he did.

At first he cried, and said he was sorry for putting us in the position of having to fend for ourselves. He wept his way back in, promising us a new life. He said he learned his lesson and would never gamble again. He had a job, and he would look after his family. He even brought some toys. My brother, Terry, was happy to see him, as he was unaware of the abuse. I was sickened by his arrival, and Jean went to her room, knowing we were trapped.

We remained on guard, and for a short time he appeared to have changed his ways. There was a local bar at the end of the street where he got a job as a bartender and would often play piano for the guests. Predictably, the peace and tranquility only lasted a few weeks before he fell back into his old ways.

But this time, I would have none of it. When my father came back into our lives, I was eleven and had gained some street smarts. Necessity being the mother of invention, we stepped off the boat and learned to live by our wits.

We were creative in our attempts to rise above our status. Jean capitalized on her looks to get odd jobs, and I used my shyness and willingness to please, running errands for harried housewives for ten cents or even a nickel.

Canada wasn't the panacea we hoped it would be. Although it was a land of immigrants, people were suspicious and unfriendly. From day one, we had our eye on America across the border, where the streets were paved with gold, and there were cowboys, apple pie and opportunity. We were going there—of that I was certain.

One day, I walked into the apartment after playing outside, and my father grabbed me from behind. He was crying as he planted slobbering kisses on my face, telling me how much he had missed me. I could smell the repulsive scent of alcohol and tobacco on his breath. I was mortified when he mentioned my eleven-year-old budding breasts, which weren't worthy of a training bra.

My earliest memory of this man was that he was very adept at catching me alone when no one else was around. Then he would put his hand under my dress, while he manipulated his body. I was so young when this first happened that for the longest time, I thought that's what every father did. He used me for his sick and perverse pleasure, and made me promise not to tell. Later on I learned that he had done the same things and worse to my sister.

Found

When I turned seven I realized this was abnormal behavior, and I became very resourceful at avoiding being alone with him. I would also never bring a friend over to the house for fear of what he would do to her.

This particular time I managed to squirm away and ran back outside, waiting until the rest of the family came home, before I ventured back. That night I felt guilty when I heard my parents shouting in their bedroom, knowing my father was taking out his frustrations and inadequacies on my mom. My siblings and I endured the embarrassing taunts and filthy language all night long.

The next morning, it was evident that my mother had been crying. My father, who was in a belligerent mood, said he was going to walk my mother to work and wait outside until she was finished. He was certain she was having a relationship with one of her dance students, and he was going to catch her in the act and beat the crap out of him.

That evening the mood in the apartment was calm. Apparently my father was appeased by his visit to the dance studio. Terry and I were playing dominos, and my mom was sewing a dance costume for an upcoming recital. Jean, who was fifteen, was on a date. She had been told to be home by eight o'clock, and when she wasn't home by a quarter past eight, I started to worry what my father would do. He was watching television, drinking a cup of coffee, and seemed disinterested in us.

Then Jean walked in the door and he exploded, yelling obscenities and filthy language that no one should hear. Jumping to his feet, he threw his coffee mug, hitting my sister on the side of her face. When the cup hit the floor, it smashed into hundreds of pieces.

"Why didn't you call to say you would be late? Who do you think you are? I am in charge around here. You are nothing but a tramp. . . a whore."

His face was contorted and his eyes were spitting hatred as he looked around the room, talking to a phantom presence that only he saw. In that moment, I saw the devil. And with that, he picked up the large phone from the table and slammed it against Jean's head.

CHAPTER SEVEN

THE PRECINCT

Was I to blame somehow?

The next few days were a blur. Terry and I stayed in the apartment, too embarrassed to venture outside, while my mother wearily went to work, to the hospital, and to the police station with Jean. On the second night, she came home in a trance. Without a word, she drank a glass of brandy, which was unusual as she disliked alcohol, and went to bed.

The next day, she told me I was going with her to the police station. When I asked why I needed to go, she said bad things had been disclosed, and I was needed as a witness.

A witness to what, I wondered? *Why wasn't Terry asked to go?* He lived in the house too.

As we emerged from the subway the following morning, the formidable Metropolitan Ontario Police Station loomed ahead. Reluctantly, I followed my mother into the antiquated building in the heart of Toronto next to old City Hall.

We approached a busy desk where we were told with a disinterested nod to take a seat. The building smelled of mothballs, disinfectant, sweat, and the defeated odor of human misery. We waited for several hours until our names were called out for the entire world to hear. My face turned a brilliant red when the officer motioned for us to follow him. My eyes darted around, and then I tripped and lurched forward. Panic set in.

_____

We entered a room where three plain-clothes detectives and a uniformed police officer, each sporting badges and buzz-cuts, stood. To a diminutive eleven-year-old, they were ten feet tall. No smiles, all business. This police and detective stuff was serious business.

"We are here to discuss charges that have been laid against Frank Gillespie, your father, a thirty-eight-year-old male who has been detained since yesterday after he reportedly entered into a scuffle with one Jean Gillespie."

A scuffle with one Jean Gillespie! Is that what you call slamming a heavy object into the side of your defenseless, fifteen-year-old child's head, resulting in a concussion and a broken eardrum?

"We have been made aware of more serious allegations in the last twenty-four hours and we are here today to get to the bottom of it."

More serious allegations? What could be more serious than a father attacking his daughter, resulting in her being admitted to the emergency room?

I felt dizzy and claustrophobic; my mouth dry and full of cotton.

Oh please, is there water somewhere?

The walls closed in as I tried to process their words and their oddly placed anger at us. Then they began asking me questions.

"How old are you? Where were you born? Where do you go to school? With whom do you live? How old is your brother? Your sister?" And then the probing questions: "Do you get along with your siblings? Do you fight? Does your sister have a boyfriend? Do your parents argue? Have you seen them get physical with one another?"

And then: "As you are aware by now, your sister has accused your father of abuse? She is concerned that you might have suffered similar treatment."

My eyes widened at this statement.

Why would Jean think that? Neither Terry nor I were ever the brunt of his anger. Yes, we witnessed the screaming, the language, and more over the years, but it was always directed at my mother and more recently at Jean.

The detective continued, "Your sister has given us a statement about your father's on-going violence. We have written and signed reports that tell of repeated mistreatment, both physical and sexual. She said she has been sexually molested by your father throughout her childhood."

A cataclysmic bomb fell from the sky annihilating everything in its path.

Smash. . .utter destruction.

SEXUAL. . .MOLESTATION. . .Oh dear God.

These men glared down at me from towering heights, and I huddled in pathetic repose. Their gazes were hardened, and one of the men chewed gum like a rat chewing through a cupboard to get inside.

My head expanded, catching the hairs in my lank pony tail, and the contents of my stomach begged relief, all to the sounds of clanging doors and hurried steps. The men waited, and a breathless stillness settled in as my heart pounded.

Please. . . please go away. Please leave me alone; I am just a kid. I don't know why I was brought here. I don't know anything. I am sorry. I won't ever be bad again.

I was sickened and alarmed by the words that were spoken. Shivering, I looked to my mother for a bit of relief. When I shot her a furtive glance, I saw that she was staring intently at me. A frown had overtaken her otherwise flawlessly composed face. My ears began to ring, and I felt like I was being swallowed up in one lascivious gulp by the giants in the room.

I begged God to help me.

"These are serious allegations young lady, and we need you to tell us if you are a victim of incest, of sexual abuse by your father. You need to speak up. These are very serious accusations."

The words incest and exploitation hung in the air, and I felt the color drain from my face.

There was no escape in sight as their question sank in.

My mother turned away and was staring at her image in the mirror across the room. Her long blonde hair cascaded onto her shoulders as she took herself in—*Shoulders back, head up,* as she would constantly lecture her students.

"Take your time in answering, Miss," Gum Chewer said.

"Can you tell us right now that you have been subjected to the sexual advances of your father?

I nodded assent and waited to die.

The note-taking cop asked me to speak up. I nodded once more. The detective asked what the nod meant. I nodded two, three or four times, trying to please. Frustrated, the detective admonished me again to speak up, to answer with a yes or a no. They were mad at me and tears welled up.

Like a schoolteacher who had just about had it with the unruly students, the gum chewer said, "Has your father ever exposed his private parts to you?"

My mother, who finally came the tiniest bit alive, gasped at the question. I sat unmoving, ashamed, head down like a ghost in the corner of the room, nodding my head, up and down, staring at my feet, hoping they would take flight and transport me out of this place. The third detective, a non-participant until this time, softly called me by my name saying, "Linda, can you tell me if you have ever been sexually molested by your father?"

"Yes," I whispered.

With that, my mother collapsed on the floor.

I have a hard time recalling in detail what happened next. There were terrible questions asked, graphic details asked and answered over a period of time.

The precinct

Over time the memory of the humiliating interrogation slowly softened around the hardened edges. It hasn't been entirely erased, just put on a shelf to be dusted off on occasion.

That was the first time I flew in the air. I recall transporting myself out of there, looking at the child below from a soft cloud. I observed the child below who was asked to view pictures of the male anatomy. I felt so very sorry for the forlorn little girl whose hands were twisting. That wasn't me. I observed her from above, out of body.

Did my mother stay through the entire ordeal? My memory fades there. At times, I was aware of her presence, always propped up on the brink of fainting once again. At other points, I remember a scrawny girl, alone with the entire male precinct population. It's best not to think about it.

CHAPTER \ EIGHT

COURT DAY

I heard the words "restraining order." I was safe for a while.

In the ensuing months while waiting for a court date, we found ourselves hiding from a man who sought revenge for our disloyalty, for the "lies" we spread; a dangerous man on the loose, who was free to roam the streets in search of us.

A year passed, and I was approaching twelve years of age; while Jean, a blossoming beauty with a newfound confidence born out of deep resentment and a smoldering anger, was seventeen.

I don't recall my mom during this time; she had her own life, a woman who put one foot in front of the other, carrying on in her British way. Chin up, shoulders back, dancing her way to her dreams.

The court date finally arrived, and we dreaded the prospect of taking part in this public display. Without conversation, nor counseling, we each silently handled our part in the unfolding story, never uttering a word to each other. It was as if by unspoken agreement, we were not giving credence to the reality. In our minds, it simply hadn't happened.

My father had a public defender, and we had the cops. As a minor, I was not allowed in the courtroom while testimony was given. I was to go in for my portion of the proceedings and leave immediately after.

When it was my turn on the witness stand, I meekly walked into the courtroom, a frightened mouse, eyes straight ahead.

Heads turned as I solemnly trudged down the aisle to take my place. The room was full. A Bible was presented. I placed my hand on it and took the oath, swearing to tell the truth and nothing but the truth, so help me God.

Questions were asked and answers were given, but it was all a blur. I had not seen my father in almost a year, and I wasn't curious now. I did not look in the direction of the table where he was seated.

My memory that day is of only two things: a judge in black robes with stern, close-set eyes boring through me.

The other, a constant wailing, "Oh my poor little girl, look at what her mother has done to our children. She has turned them against me."

Admonished by the judge, my father resorted to quiet sobs. The court date lasted just one day. No witnesses were brought in other than our unfortunate family.

We must not have been convincing, because in the end, he was portrayed by his assigned defense lawyer to be the victim of a jealous and sick woman who orchestrated a preposterous story and elicited the help of her daughters because she wanted to be free to date other men. With a slap on the hand for giving Jean a concussion and breaking her eardrum, they let him go.

CHAPTER NINE

DEPORTATION

It turned out that we needed help sooner than expected.

While hiding out once more, our family was featured in a tabloid magazine, and my new little friend from school told me that she was not allowed to play with me again. I didn't blame her. I was a pariah.

Eventually, one of my mother's many admirers set her up in her own small business that she owned and operated. Lilian's was a lovely dance studio, and my mother's former students flocked there to take lessons. Ultimately it became successful and lifted us out of poverty.

With my father on the loose, we were constantly on the run. We moved into the home of a big, happy Polish family who let us rent their basement after learning of our plight. They were outcasts themselves, immigrants who fled their country at a time of civil strife, and they were delighted to be able to help and protect us.

This lovely family had suffered greatly in their native Poland, and they were now proud Canadians. Like most homes in this ethnically diverse part of town, their front porch had on display a large Canadian maple leaf flag.

We loved our life here. Everyone was from somewhere else and had funny accents. There were many backyard get-togethers and lots of camaraderie. We found ourselves smiling for the first time in a long while as life took on a rhythm of peace, tranquility and normalcy.

Bob-cha, the family matriarch, a wizened old grandmother who spoke little English, would often invite us to share delicious home-cooked meals. In broken English, the family regaled us with stories and laughter, and we danced the polka while the patriarch played a poor rendition of "Beer Barrel Polka" on the accordion.

In return, my mother delighted in teaching them the Viennese Waltz as she whirled out of the kitchen and into the hallway, down the steps, and into the small garden. This was a time of laughter and happiness.

But it would be short lived.

On a warm summer day, three months after the trial, Jean received a phone call from our father, who had tracked down the phone number of our host family. When she got on the line, he spewed hate-filled vitriol. His not-guilty verdict had inflamed his confidence, and he told Jean he was free, free to destroy our lives. He said was coming for us. He had our address and the name and phone number of the landlord. He said he would find us and kill us.

We had wrongly assumed that while our father was a bully, a pervert, a wife beater, he was too much of a coward to be a killer. We did believe, however, that he could show up at any time and embarrass us.

Our kind and gentle landlords wanted us to stay rather than run. They suggested we draw a line in the sand, confront him, and call him out for being the bully that he was.

Jean, who was no longer a victim, agreed. Although slight in build, she was certain she could murder him with her bare hands. Jean also had a detective friend who was infatuated with her, who promised to help if she needed him to. When Jean told him what transpired on the phone, he offered to drive by the house with his partner at the end of his shift.

As fate would have it, at the end of a beautiful summer day, two plain-clothes detectives drove down the street in an unmarked car and spotted my father walking toward our home. They pulled over, deciding to deal with him right there.

They stopped him and said he would face jail time if they ever saw him anywhere near us again. They were shocked when they found out he was carrying a gun and likely on his way to kill us.

That incident could have ended our lives; instead it was a new beginning for us. As a non-citizen of Canada on a visiting visa, he was booked for possession of an unregistered firearm and deportation proceedings started immediately. That was the last we heard from our father.

It was the first time I encountered the power of deportation, and fortunately it was to our benefit. In the not too distant future, deportation proceedings would shake me to the core and foment a life of activism resulting in consequences I could not possibly imagine.

For now, all I cared about was that my pervert father was sent back to England, and I, at twelve years of age, was free to live my life.

CHAPTER TEN

ICE FOLLIES

She thought she might have punched and kicked him
but wasn't sure.

It was amazing that my sister, who never had the benefit of a skating coach, landed a job as an ice dancer with the Ice Follies when she was seventeen years old. Jean had a natural talent. She was one of those enviable people born with the ability to sing, dance, act and skate, and when she made her mind up to do something, she did it to perfection.

I was so happy for her. After surviving so much heartache and suffering much more abuse at the hands of our father than I did, my sister was achieving her dream.

On my thirteenth birthday, Jean sent me a bus ticket and an invitation to spend the weekend with her in Detroit, Michigan, where she would be performing for ten days in the traveling Ice Follies. With passport in hand, I crossed from

Canada into the U.S. at the Windsor/Detroit border. I had no idea that future crossings would prove to be the bane of my existence.

Watching the show, I knew I wanted to be in show business come hell or high water. It was a magical life reserved for a very few, and I wanted in.

A natural camaraderie existed amongst the skaters. They looked out for each other as life on the road often meant long months away from loved ones.

The Detroit arena where the Ice Follies was playing was walking distance from the hotel, but the company strongly cautioned the cast and crew to always walk in groups.

On the night of my arrival, following the show, our assemblage strolled arm in arm past a small alley when suddenly a dark figure shot out of the shadows, wrestled Jean's purse from her hand and ran back into the darkness. Stunned, we all stood mouths agape, not comprehending what had just happened. Then Jean bolted into the alley in hot pursuit.

Witnessing her outbursts of anger over the years, I knew she would not take it lightly being a victim. I also knew that at 110 pounds she would be no match for a seasoned thief, which was why I was so horrified that she was running full pelt down a dark alley in chase of a crook.

Her friends were panicked and shouted for her to come back, while I begged them to go after her.

The male dancers, although fit and healthy, were not scrappers. They knew they could lose their livelihood if they suffered a broken bone, yet several of them cautiously headed into the entrance of the alley. Before they could take more than a few tentative steps, a lone figure could be glimpsed emerging from the shadows, running in our direction.

Materializing with her purse held tight, Jean sprinted past us, then glanced back, and yelled for us to follow. It was several blocks before we caught up to my sister, who had finally stopped and was trying to regain her composure. Her hands were on her knees as she panted, and there was a sickly but triumphant smile plastered on her face. With eyes blazing, she spurted out what had just transpired in that dark alley.

She said it hadn't taken long for her to catch up to the thief, who no doubt was shocked to see such a small figure chasing after him. Blinded by rage, she launched herself onto his back, knocking him off balance, causing them both to fall.

Jean thought she smacked him. . .yes, she smacked him hard once or twice. She thought she might have also punched and kicked him, but she couldn't remember—it was all a blur. Wrenching the purse from his grip, she ran back to the safety of her friends.

We stood in silence, mouths agape, spellbound.

In the end, the incident went unreported to the police, and more importantly to the show management. If the Follies executives got wind of Jean running into an alley to pursue a thief, she could be subject to a potential suspension for behavior unbecoming of a company member.

The following day word quickly spread among the performers, and peals of laughter could be heard throughout the hotel.

That afternoon, before leaving for the show, excited cast members arrived with the *Detroit Free Press* newspaper in hand. Inside was a story of a man beaten and left for dead in an alley late last night. He was transported to the hospital with a concussion and various other injuries. The article asked anyone with information to call the number posted. It was thought the attack was gang-related.

The cast members closed in around Jean and our little band of witnesses like members of a secret society. They would never breathe a word about this incident. But that night, as the cast swirled and skated past Jean, on each axel, jump, camel spin, and synchronized group move, giggling could be heard throughout the arena, much to the consternation of the show director.

Jean was a fighter, and it was payback time once again for all the abuse suffered at the hands of our father. I looked up to her and wanted to be her, but I was just her shadow. Maybe one day I would find the strength she had attained. Strength meant perseverance.

CHAPTER ELEVEN

THE CELLO

He likes me. . . he really likes me.

From the time I could walk, I could dance. My mother may not have been invested in her children excelling in school, but she made sure that we could dance and skate.

By now, Jean had joined the Ice Follies in the U.S. My brother, Terry, who never knew about the abuse his two sisters endured, was confused about why his father left Canada. He received letters from England, telling him that we had fabricated stories so that our mother could be free to take up with other men. Although Terry witnessed violent bursts of anger, he was the youngest child and close to his father. He became angry, accusing us of causing the deportation. He refused to believe his father was intent on killing us. And so, in less than a year he went to join him.

With Terry in England and Jean traveling the world, it was just me and my mom, and most often I was on my own. My mother had her own dance studio, dance competitions, and costumes to supervise.

At thirteen I was adrift, awkward, insecure, and like a ghost, I generally went unnoticed.

On Tuesdays and Thursdays, I carried my cello home because the music teacher wanted me to practice every waking moment. He was frustrated because when he called upon me to perform even the smallest of musical tasks, I would screech away on my instrument causing comic relief in the classroom.

On cello days, I would attempt to take the streetcar home rather than slog through the street, but I was embarrassed because the driver and the fellow passengers begrudged the space that my instrument took.

I remember my first and only high school crush was the drummer in the school band. He was genetically perfect like a Nordic god with fair skin, a perfect aquiline nose, piercing black eyes, and wavy hair.

Unbeknownst to him, I would get to music class early so that I had the best seat from which to observe him through the string section. He was the main attraction in my nightly dreams. From time to time, I would catch his eye, imagining a small smile, a nod in my direction, but I knew there wasn't a snowball's chance in hell that he found me interesting.

One morning, I got to class late. Walking in with a crimson face, I saw that my usual seat was missing, which meant I had to search for a chair. Then, oh heart of hearts. . . my beautiful Nordic god gallantly strode over to an empty chair in the back of the room, retrieved it just for me, and placed it in the middle of the string section with a flourish. I was over the moon. The most popular boy in the entire school was demonstrating my value to the entire class. Blushing from head to toes, I gratefully and self-consciously made my way toward the seat, my cello banging into my classmates.

He likes me.

But as I started to sit down, he whipped the chair out from underneath me, and I fell to the ground, my cello falling onto the girl in the next seat.

Not only did my love interest not have eyes for me, he apparently hated me. I was so blinded by his beauty that I had failed to notice earlier signs of his propensity for cruelty.

Tears formed as I struggled to my feet, and I saw the hatred in his eyes as he sneered and said, "All's fair in love and war. And this is war."

The cello

The entire classroom erupted in uproarious laughter, and the irritated teacher rapped his baton on a music stand.

I look back on this incident with such sadness, not just for the young girl who received more than her share of abuse and oppression, but for every unfortunate child who is the target of a bully.

Thinking back, I am aware of an early resolve that crept into my soul. A storm was brewing—a seething, relentless anger was setting in. I did not want to be defined by these random happenings in my life.

It was only much later that I realized all those setbacks and hardships were my training ground, opportunities that made me strong, that I could learn from and transcend, so that one day I would be prepared for success and ready to make my mark on the world.

CHAPTER TWELVE

THE SALESLADY, 1960

I was not worthy of her attention.

I was excited, as I headed downtown to the big, beautiful Toronto Eaton Center, home to over 250 of the best shops in the heart of the city.

I had saved my own money by doing odd chores for the family upstairs, and today I was going to buy my first brand-new lipstick with the cash I had carefully tucked away in my little plastic purse,

This was a special occasion. No more borrowing remnant lipsticks from my mother and sister. I planned to search every store until I found exactly what I was looking for.

I imagined sauntering up to the counter at one of the department stores, confident, head held high, judiciously selecting just the right shade of lipstick in a shiny case. I would use it to impress others whenever I could. I had four dollars for this purchase and a dollar for the round-trip subway excursion.

After several hours of display case shopping, I was ready to buy. I had found the perfect purchase that with tax would add up to less than four dollars, which would allow me to sit at a counter and enjoy a cup of tea, while applying my new lipstick.

At the counter was a beautifully groomed saleswoman with an air of grace and charm. I admired her elegance and waited patiently, making eye contact whenever I could. I was excited to be in this grand store with money in hand about to conduct business.

I watched her glide up and down the counter clicking her high heels, busily rearranging and adjusting the displays while she kept her eye out for potential customers who were much more important than me. I stood there for quite some time, trying to get her attention as she went by, but she was clearly avoiding me.

I stood silently by with lipstick in hand, my arm out-stretched displaying the money; but she had obviously made up her mind that I was not worthy of her attention.

Humiliated, I took stock of myself, trying to imagine how I looked through her eyes. I was wearing a tatty sweater, scuffed shoes, socks that refused to stay up, and I was hold-ing a tacky plastic purse.

I willed myself not to cry, but tears filled my eyes. I was sick and tired of the meanness and abuse I had endured for as long as I could remember.

But I was no longer that meek, insecure, person. After my father left, I had resolved to never be exploited again. I had worked so hard to raise myself up from that other Linda. Damn it, I was worthy of a new tube of lipstick.

And then the moment that would forever change the tra-jectory of my life happened. She waved me away with a big grand gesture. I couldn't' believe she had just dismissed me with the fluff of her hand. Perhaps I wasn't as imperceptible, as invisible as I thought.

A slow crimson burn started at my toes and moved slowly upwards, through my body, into my chest, and exploded inside my head. I felt a mounting, boiling rage.

A couple of customers much more worthy of the clerk's attention strolled up to the counter to look at the perfumes on display, and she rushed toward them as though she couldn't get there fast enough. I watched her fawn over these two new arrivals and conspiratorially roll her eyes in my direction as they nodded and looked on.

Then something amazing and life-changing happened in that store in the most famous shopping center in Canada.

I grew several feet taller, and the tears that had so recently filled my eyes melted away as I erupted. Observing the group with a fierce loathing, I roared:

"AM I BOTHERING YOU? I want to buy this lipstick. Why won't you help me?"

Everyone around me was silent. You could hear a pin drop. A commotion in that kind of establishment was unheard of.

Empowered, I shouted again. **"I have been standing here for half an hour, and you have ignored me. WHY? I just want to buy this lipstick!"**

As though the store was on fire and her life depended on it, the clerk quickly ran to my side of the counter. Her face was now a bright hue of red much like my lipstick choice, as she put her finger to her lips admonishing me to be silent. But I was having none of it. It felt like I was ten feet tall as I stared her down.

I don't know where this other Linda came from. All I know is that she was here now, and she was in charge. The clerk stood in front of me, her cold eyes imploring me with expressions of anger, confusion, and then, to my delight, despair.

This young girl, this lesser being, had challenged this woman with her smart shoes and well-coiffed hair. I had disrupted her perfect world. And yet, I saw in her eyes that she was looking at me with a new respect. Without uttering a word, she pleaded with me to please calm down, as she grabbed the lipstick with shaking hands, and quickly began the transaction.

Approaching at lightning speed from across the store, a man possessing an aura of responsibility, wearing a natty business suit complete with a red bow tie, came to a halt in front of me. He was quite obviously the manager of this great establishment. He towered over me as the customers and clerks alike stood absolutely quiet, waiting, watching for something catastrophic to happen.

"Is something wrong?" he loudly inquired. "What was the reason for that outburst?" He was about to scold me. But to his chagrin, my alter ego took him on, too.

"ARE YOU TELLING ME OFF, TOO? I JUST WANTED TO BUY THIS LIPSTICK WITH THIS MONEY, AND SHE WOULDN'T SERVE ME! WHAT IS WRONG WITH YOU PEOPLE?"

I said this with an authority that was not part of my usual demeanor. Instinctively, I knew this was a defining moment. I knew that if I backed down now, I would forever be banished to the back of the room, to a life of subservience to these superior human beings.

At this point a security guard was heading our way, speaking into a walkie-talkie.

Damn. Now what?

Faltering a bit, I considered my options while standing my ground. Had I done something wrong in coming here? Was this place reserved only for people of a certain class or considerable wealth? No. My money was as good as anyone else's in this store. I had worked hard for these dollars and cents.

Don't back down now, Linda. You set this scene in motion; see it through. You did nothing wrong.

As I was contemplating my next move, a beautiful, refined woman in a fur coat strode purposefully into the fray. She stood between me, the guard, and the manager.

Turning to me, she asked, "Are you okay? Are these people scaring you? What can I do to help?"

Her warm brown eyes were full of concern. Large diamonds adorned her hands and ears, and she wore her hair in a classic upsweep topped off with a stylish hat.

Softly she asked again, "Are you trying to purchase an item and they won't take your money, dear?"

With trembling lips and some of my confidence ebbing, I stuttered, "I just wanted to buy this lipstick."

She bent down, her lovely hand enveloped mine, and she asked my name. Then she confidently pushed past the manager and the guard, and confronted the clerk. In a commanding, authoritative voice, she said, "Wrap this up for Linda, please, and give her a nice bag to put it in."

It was amazing.

Once the transaction was complete, she released my hand and turned to face me. Leaning down so that her words were spoken directly to me, but loud enough for the others to hear, she dispatched a message I will never forget.

"You have chosen a beautiful lipstick. Good choice, well done. This is one of my favorites, too. Do you know that you are a strong and clever girl, Linda? You are, and the world is full of people who will stand in your way. Don't EVER let anyone make you feel like you are less worthy than they are. Now, with your head held high, take your parcel, and be on your way."

Trembling, I thanked her, took my package, and walked slowly through the store with my head held high, never looking back. I could feel all eyes on me, but things were different now. I was no longer the ragamuffin who first entered this establishment. I was strong, I was clever, I had just been validated.

I left that place a changed person. That incident transformed me and changed the way I lived my life forevermore. I was no longer going to be a victim. I was the captain of my own ship, and I was going to direct it on a course for success. I would never be taken advantage of again. I would never be that sad little girl again.

CHAPTER THIRTEEN

THE SWEATER

I was an even more peculiar object than before.

My sister Jean, who had a glamourous job and earned a regular paycheck, would routinely send money home. One time, when I was fifteen, a beautiful baby-blue cashmere sweater arrived. I was midway through school, which I hated, and saving every penny I could earn working odd jobs. I delivered newspapers in the early morning hours; on Friday nights I worked in a photo lab hand cutting negatives; and on weekends I babysat. Over a full school year I saved $85 that I stashed in a jar under my bed.

The sweater was too beautiful to wear for everyday occasions, but those were the only occasions available to me. One day, feeling brave and even a little bit pretty, I decided to take it out of the tissue paper it was preserved in, and wear it to school.

I felt good about myself that fateful morning—my long hair was pulled into a bouncy ponytail with matching blue ribbon; my books were tied together with a piece of the same ribbon, and I even managed to find a pair of blue bobby sox. As I strode confidently onto the school yard, I thought I might even catch the eye of a boy.

The sweater and I immediately drew the attention of the school's most popular girls. These were the pretty girls, the mean girls, the girls who snickered as the awkward guys walked past, wore bored expressions and rolled their eyes contemptuously when ignored by the handsome jocks. Each of them was blessed with good looks and attire that can only be attributed to a charmed life and overachieving parents.

I was skinny, had freckles, limp hair, and typically wore ill-fitting, handmade clothes. I tried in vain to fit in when I started secondary school at the Harbord Collegiate Institute in Toronto, and I was beginning to lose the British accent.

I worked on holding my head up high and my shoulders back. I tried to be direct and welcoming. I studied hard and tried to be one of the "admired girls."

No one here knew the sordid story of my father. I thought that if I excelled in theater, ice skating, and dance, I would attract friends. Instead, my abilities in these areas drew the ire of the popular girls.

On the day I wore the cashmere sweater to school, I soon found myself encircled by kids spewing hate.

Didn't I know skinny girls with freckles and accents were inferior? Why was I pretending to be someone I wasn't? Why didn't I go back to the country I came from? It didn't matter what I wore; I was a hopeless case. I was certain to be a thief. I should take the garment off now.

With that, they proceeded to pull at me, grabbing my hair, yanking at the sweater. This happened while a schoolyard full of students stood back and watched, grateful they weren't the one being bullied. It was clear to me that no one was going to come to my rescue.

Then, just like in the department store, the most amazing thing happened. Without warning, a seething anger bubbled up inside of me; and I drew my arm back and slammed my fist into the face of the main tormentor, knocking her to the ground. I was as shocked as she was and stood panting with my hands balled into fists, waiting for the next opponent.

Who else wants a fist in the face?

I wondered where that came from. I had weak wrists and couldn't even open the screw top of a soda bottle. I had never hit anyone in my life, and here I was punching one of the popular girls and waiting for the next one.

I was dragged into the principal's office, and when no parent came to claim me, I was sent home with a note and a three-month suspension.

As the years passed, it became clear to me that there were two Lindas. There was the indefatigable Linda, who chugged along full of optimism and resolve, who sought kindness and was on a quest to make the world a better, gentler place for all.

I didn't want to think about the other Linda who scared me.

And yet the suspension from school was one of the best things that happened to me. I got a job at a local gym— cleaning equipment, washing towels, and helping the trainers. One of the trainers who knew my sister, Jean, talked to the manager, who agreed to pay me fifty cents an hour and let me use all the equipment after hours.

I owe a lot to that trainer whose name I sadly can't recall. From the moment I set foot in the gym, she told me I had potential, remarking at my prowess as a dancer when she saw me practicing after hours in front of the large mirrors, moving to the music. I stayed at the gym as long as I wanted since my mother was busy with her own life and didn't care what I did.

The trainer told me I was pretty, which I had never heard before. Quite the opposite, I always thought I was ugly. Released from the daily constraints of having to go to school where I was bullied, I experienced a new found freedom. As soon as my head hit the pillow at night, I flew, soaring through the skies, envisioning the person I was supposed to be, looking forward to a new life,

I made my way to the gym each day feeling empowered and euphoric. This was a different Linda. I was no longer a loser; I was making money. Not much, but it was mine. I also had the gym to myself at the end of each day and I took full advantage of all it had to offer.

Two weeks after the school suspension, I turned sixteen. On my birthday I decided to take some of the money I had earned that was stashed under my bed and splurge on my first hair salon visit. What a transformation it was when I came out of the salon with long blonde tresses.

Eventually I signed on as a model with the Jerry Lodge Talent Agency and began making the rounds and going on dance auditions. I soon bagged a big prize. It was the '60s when go-go and disco dancing were the rage. Pepsi was looking for a wholesome, energetic, young blonde dancer to be the face of Diet Pepsi, and I was the perfect fit. Suddenly I was making good money.

When the three-month suspension ended, I returned to school driving an Austin Healy Sprite. My mother's newest love interest was the manager at a car dealership, and he arranged for the purchase of this used gem.

I pulled into the school parking lot each day where only a few other cars owned by students were parked. Yet despite this privileged social status, I still didn't fit in. In fact, I felt even more isolated. I came back to school thinking the confident Linda would now be accepted and surrounded by newly-acquired friends, but that wasn't the case.

The sweater

Canadians are reserved by nature, and adhere to certain social rules. They are nice and polite, but they aren't exuberantly friendly. I didn't fit into the mold or the image they were used to, and so I was looked upon as even more peculiar than before the suspension. Within a month, I left school permanently.

CHAPTER FOURTEEN

DANCING GIRL

Whoa! I feel good, I knew that I would, now.
—James Brown

After leaving high school just six weeks short of graduation to take modeling assignments, I heard about an open dance audition for a soon-to-be televised variety show called *It's Happening*.

I was seventeen years old; I had friends, a sporty car, and plenty of dates; and I was ready for a new challenge. The audition took place over two days in a large rehearsal hall in downtown Toronto.

Although I had achieved a modicum of success with bit parts in commercials, walk-on spots on television, and some modeling, I was hungry for a regular paycheck. I wanted a secure position where I could develop my dancing and acting skills and "be someone." My sister and I had changed our given names shortly after our father was jailed, and I took the stage name Linda Christopher.

Standing in the middle of a long line of dancers, I took it all in. Ahead of and behind me were ballerinas dressed in pretty tutus with their hair pulled back into the requisite buns on their heads," and their Moms on hand to ease their angst. These were seasoned young ladies, girls who made the rounds, who went from audition to audition, who spent years perfecting a dance form that required expensive training and imparted grace and precision. And then there were the few oddballs like me.

I was a self-taught, free-style dancer. My education came from years as a child dancing on my mother's ballroom circuit. The girls here, who were veterans at auditioning, knew what to do, how to act, what to wear, who to bring. They looked like ballerina Barbie dolls – with pretty ribbons adorning their locks, wearing full stage makeup.

It was intimidating. I didn't fit in. I had the wrong "look." I had cutoff jeans and a mid-waist T-shirt on, and two giant ponytails that stuck out of each side of my head. The moms eyed me suspiciously like I was a freak.

I would have run from the scene, but I craved the opportunity to be a dancer on what was certain to be a Canadian hit TV variety show that everyone was calling Canada's answer to *American Bandstand.*

Eventually the long line wound its way down the street into the theater, and I could at last catch a glimpse of the audition process.

The dancers, grouped in tens, each displayed a paper sign with a number on it that was handed to them when they came in the door. I was number 307.

We were told we would be called in groups to the stage and then we would sit in a semi-circle while each hopeful dancer performed a routine to the music of their choice. We had ninety seconds to make a positive impression.

Some of the entrants were good and others not too good. Many were seasoned ballerinas who held their heads high while en pointe, who gave their all as they danced to music more suited for the Sugar Plum Fairies.

I thought there was little imagination here, or did I get the whole thing wrong? When asked a question, they each responded in the same little voice. I noted the judges whispering, shaking their heads slightly. There was very little conversation with the girls once they completed their set except to say "Thank you" and "We will get back to you in a couple of days, once we have completed the auditions."

And then it was my turn. My heart pounded out of my chest as I took center stage, certain I had chosen an inappropriate tune. I knew I didn't fit in with the general tone of the day, but I was confident in my abilities.

I chose the James Brown number, "I Feel Good." Right or wrong this was my music. As the first chord hit, the audience sat up in shock. Well, here goes EVERYTHING! I transformed myself into an uninhibited, provocative, frenzied street dancer, improvising as I shook, shimmied, and flew through the air.

I feel good. . .So good. . .so good. . .I got you. .

Just like that, ninety seconds was over. I stood waiting to be laughed off the stage. Instead, a miracle happened. I was asked to stay on stage and continue my audition.

On fire, I exuberantly flew across the stage, head and pigtails moving side to side. At "so good, so good," my entire body struck a stilled and studied pose. On the upbeat, I flew with abandon once more. No matter what came of this moment, I did it on my terms. It was exhilarating. Ears roaring and heart racing, I imagined enthusiastic roars of approval. Yes—it was true. They were cheering for me. The louder the shouts, the more I shimmied and jumped. When the performance was over, I stood panting, hands on hips ready to do it all over again.

Then the show's director stood up and in an Irish brogue he said, "Congratulations. You are our first dancer chosen. See you at rehearsal."

I did it. I was guaranteed a spot. Thank you, James Brown, King of Soul.

In an instant, my future was secure.

This time in my life was one for the story books.

Untrained dancer makes good.

My former alma mater even posted a story on the school's bulletin board: "Graduate of Harbord Collegiate Institute finds fame and fortune on hit television show." Just like that, I was a graduate.

As a dancer on a hit TV show, I was sought out for extra work, including bookings at respected nightclubs, industry dinner performances, TV commercials, and fashion shows. I was asked to participate in charitable events and was intrigued by the generosity of showbiz folks. With a nationally televised variety show and bit parts in movies, I was living the dream. I was the Diet Pepsi girl, a Chrysler spokesmodel, and model for Du Pont of Canada and the Hudson Bay Company.

I even received fan mail, and was invited by the entire graduating class of a private boys' school to be their prom date. But most odd, long before Suzanne Somers' hairdo became popular when she appeared on the hit TV show, "Three's Company in 1977, the "Linda Christopher" hairstyle with long bangs and two platinum blonde pigtails was the rage across Canada.

We always expected Jean to be successful. Surprisingly, I was too. It was an exciting time as I blossomed from a whimpering non-entity to a self-assured young woman with an eye on a successful career in show business and eventual stardom.

I would meet my future husband when he appeared on the show, kick-starting a career in entertainment that would lead me to the stage and the homes of celebrities.

But most significant, I would discover something crucial about myself—if I set a goal and didn't waver, I could achieve anything.

CHAPTER \ FIFTEEN

GLENN

I bid goodbye to my Canadian life and set off for Sin City.

I met Glenn Smith in 1967 through friend and renowned restaurateur Gordon Josie, who also operated the Friars Club, one of the most popular nightclubs in Canada. My weekly television show, *It's Happening,* was booked at the Friars Club for a one-week special engagement.

In the audience on closing night was a Canadian group, called Glenn Smith and the Fables, who had just returned from a one year tour of the U.S. Touted as one of the most successful groups to come out of Canada, they were the next act scheduled to perform at the club.

Glenn and I were each successful in our own right—he as a musician and singer; me a dancer, model, and actress. When we first met, I was the lead dancer on *It's Happening,* and Glenn was performing all over the world. He had recently been named Canadian Entertainer of the Year.

As a child prodigy, Glenn mastered every instrument and played many of them in his shows. He was talented, handsome, and possessed a great stage presence and sense of humor that the audience loved. At every show beautiful women slipped him their phone numbers, making it very clear they found him attractive.

Glenn was also a recording artist, and in the early 1980s, he and longtime friends Gladys Knight and the Pips, released a song titled "Forever Yesterday." The song was written and produced by Glenn, who joined Gladys and the Pips in performing the vocals. All proceeds from the sale of the song were dedicated to the benefit and memory of the twenty-eight children who were murdered over a two year period by serial killer Wayne Williams, in what became known as "The Atlanta Child Murders."

I was drawn to Glenn as much by his kindness as his on-stage prowess. But I had sworn to myself that I would never marry. No man would ever hurt me again. As a local celebrity, I enjoyed the attention of many of the city's most eligible bachelors, and am not proud that I felt a certain satisfaction in turning down their offers of dates.

When I met Glenn, I was moving in an intoxicating circle, not expecting to fall for a Canadian entertainer. I had set my sights on stardom, perhaps joining Jean, who was under contract at Universal Studios in Hollywood. At the time Jean was engaged to Canadian impressionist Rich Little, and the doors were opening for both of us.

Traveling from Toronto to Hollywood between modeling and dancing assignments on a somewhat regular basis, I planned my life in five-year increments: first conquer the Toronto market, next head to Hollywood for fame and fortune next, and then move triumphantly back to the English countryside and buy the manor I imagined in my childhood.

Glenn

Marriage was not in the equation. I was having too much fun breaking hearts in the fast lane. My past was my past, and I had a newfound confidence. I was in demand, traveling between the U.S. and Canada, living an exciting life.

Unexpectedly, I was instantly smitten by a guy who didn't seem to have the slightest interest in me. Glenn and his band shared the same stage alternating shows with *It's Happening*. As I danced, I stole glances of him, and found it frustrating that he would watch for a while then turn away and join in the laughter and good times around him, seemingly forgetting about me.

I found excuses to go to his dressing room, and he would act as though I didn't exist. It exasperated me that he was always surrounded by attractive women, and I began to play the same game. I stopped watching his shows and made sure there was always an admirer waiting at the stage door at the end of the night. I was dating a prominent young attorney at the time, and I took advantage of this poor guy's affection in a ploy to elicit a reaction from Glenn.

It turned out neither of us had marriage in mind. On our first date, which was six months in the making with plenty of games played on both parts, we found out that we both admired each other's independence. We liked being masters of our own universe with no one to answer to except ourselves. I was making enough money to take care of my mother, and she and I lived in a penthouse apartment in the heart of the city. I tried to save as much money as I could. I didn't do drugs or drink alcohol. My only vice was Cadbury's milk chocolate.

My independence intrigued Glenn as his did me. Inevitably, we fell in love. Even though we were living nomadic lives apart, we agreed we each had found our soulmate, and it was time to take the next step. We would keep our careers and find a way to make it work. I finally accepted Glenn's marriage proposal and began making plans for a splashy showbiz wedding. I had no idea that marrying him would dramatically change my life.

Glenn had just been named the "Canadian Entertainer of the Year," and I had captured the prize. We would travel and eventually settle in Las Vegas, an unimagined life in an unimaginable city. Glenn had already put down roots in that crazy place, and there were big jobs there for him. He had celebrity friends who would open doors. I could find work as a model and jump on a one-hour flight to Hollywood if and when opportunities presented themselves.

The wedding was celebrated, even filmed by Canadian television, and I bid goodbye to my Canadian life as we set off for Sin City.

Once in Las Vegas, I immersed myself in the local scene but quickly found myself out in the cold. This was a much different place for a former dancer of a wholesome variety show geared to teens. I recall going on an audition for *Follies Bergere* and running out of the showroom before I made a fool of myself.

I signed up with a local modeling agency and settled into a routine of convention work, an occasional bit part in one of the many movies shot on location in the hotels, and once in a while appearing in Glenn's show. It was fun, but unfulfilling.

I worked days and Glenn worked nights and I found myself in the audience each evening stifling yawns, knowing I had to be up the next day for interviews. Women in the audience threw themselves at my husband, and I must admit it bothered me more than I thought it would. I naively thought the five band members and the three female backup singers would keep an eye out for me and protect my husband from all the offers of good times. Eventually, I stopped going to the shows and settled into a less than desirable modeling career, while Glenn stayed out until the wee hours.

Soon after our marriage, Glenn's career took off with appearances on the late-night shows, including the *Tonight*

Show with Johnny Carson and the *Merv Griffin Show*. Our friend Wayne Newton, who was known as "The Midnight Idol" and "Mr. Las Vegas," was playing to sold-out audiences and Glenn was often his opening act.

Wayne was a generous friend, and he shared the limelight with Glenn. They had both climbed their way up from the days when they performed downtown at the old Fremont Hotel. Wayne was an in-demand celebrity with shows booked years in advance, but he didn't forget his friend Glenn. Instead, they often worked together in main showrooms in Las Vegas, around the country, and across the continent entertaining the troops. Wayne was one of the most unique and talented performers of his time, and he had no qualms about following Glenn's standing ovations.

We settled into an interesting life in Las Vegas. Our friends tended to be cocktail servers, bartenders, lounge performers, celebrities, craps dealers, and hookers, plus the occasional "hanger on" fan. Our visiting family and friends went gaga over the Las Vegas excess. They were delighted to visit Liberace's home or Wayne's Casa De Shenandoah Ranch.

Glenn worked nights, and in the afternoon our home became party central filled with locals of every ilk jamming around the piano or playing pool. One day I arrived home after working a convention and there on the balcony overlooking the backyard were the Four Pips minus Gladys.

We had a boat and spent the summer months floating on Lake Mead, diving into the cool, deep water with the impressive Hoover Dam as a backdrop. We would dock the boat at the nude beach, a location kept secret from the general population, where some of the most beautiful showgirls would be stretched out bare-breasted on the sand, as magnificent Desert Big Horn sheep cast a wary eye.

In the winter, we went skiing at Lee Canyon, which was a forty-five-minute drive from downtown Las Vegas. At times, we would ski the Canyon in the morning and water ski on

Lake Mead in the afternoon. The bare breasts could be seen at Lee Canyon too, as the cold, dry weather and warm sun made for some special weather conditions. Everyone took it in stride.

As entertainers, Glenn and I found ourselves involved in many of the local charities. Glenn would appear in every Jerry Lewis telethon and a myriad of others. We were fully invested in the fabric of the city we loved. We worked, we played, and we contributed to society, but we had no idea how involved I would personally become in the charitable sector, or how much support we ourselves would one day need.

CHAPTER SIXTEEN

AND THE BAND STUTTERED ON

We laughed for three hundred miles.

Glenn Smith and the Fables were four Canadian-born high school friends brought together through an intriguing commonality. They were musically talented; they fit the suits that had already been purchased for the prior band members; they were all named Jim, Jimmy or James (with the exception of Glenn); and they each possessed a unique disfluency. . .they stuttered. In fact, they met each other in speech therapy class in high school.

We all have disfluencies in our speech ("uh," "um," "er"), but it is only considered a stutter when the impediment occurs more than ten percent of the time. Our band members were stutterers one hundred percent of the time. Although each band member stuttered, they played their instruments and sang flawlessly and were a much respected and sought-after traveling band.

Drummer Jimmy stuttered his Bs. . ."*I think the bu-bu-bu-bus is coming,*" accompanied by a hard blinking of the eyes. The bass player stammered over certain phrases, for example "*Can......................I come with you?*

Our talented singer, saxophonist and guitar player, Jimmy, had a severe and unique stutter. This speech disorder was a one of a kind, involuntary pursing of the lips into a sucking, kissing, repetitive smooch. "*Pupppwwwwpwww-puuuppppww...Hi, how are you?*"

This handsome and gifted musical genius possessed the worst speech impediment most people had ever encountered, which led to many uncomfortable stutter interventions, as people presumed they were about to receive a full-on, wet, sloppy, passionate kiss. The more Jimmy attempted to make himself understood, the more agitated he became, resulting in a prolonged stutter smooch that was amazing to witness. If you filled in the anticipated comment in hopes of alleviating his and your own discomfort, he would invariably start over again, which was excruciatingly painful to watch.

It was disconcerting for strangers, who sometimes laughed and then proceeded to imitate him, thinking they were expected to join in. Consider this: if someone came up to you and started making kissing noises, would you assume they had a speech impediment or that they were asking for some smooches?

To those of us who knew and loved Jimmy and admired his courage, it was amusing. Often we stepped into the middle of a sputtering altercation with a cautioning reproach to a potential heckler.

Although afflicted with this unusual speaking pattern, onstage Jimmy played and sang to perfection. He stuttered his entire life and came to terms with the issue, making up for this affliction by becoming a sought-after musician and entertainer. He certainly was not shy, and his impediment, although unnerving at first, did not take away from his ability to attract beautiful women.

Jimmy owned a small tape recorder that he used to record songs and stories with a positive message that he listened to when he was traveling alone on long road trips. He was very private about these tapes and never played them in front of anyone.

After borrowing our car one day, Jimmy inadvertently left one of his tapes in the recorder. Instead of a motivational tape, it was Jimmy's attempt at self-healing. It started with him proclaiming, "I will not *puppppwwwwwwwwww*." Then a sigh, a "SHIT" then "*puppwwww*...not... pupppwww... DAMN....stutter!"

Glenn and I laughed for three hundred miles.

Extended engagements across North America were our way of life for three years, and it was a blast. Each journey began when the bags were stowed, the snacks purchased, and the driver chosen. The choice of driver depended on who was the least tired, or the most tanked-up on caffeine. Each trip was highly anticipated. We started out telling jokes and stories to fill the time, and then the snacks ran out and boredom set in.

Glenn and his stuttering band were my family. Not your typical family, but they were mine, and as the days and the miles clicked away, we amassed crazy stories of life on the road.

Upon arriving at any town and venue, we were inevitably greeted by former lovers, hangers on, and remnants from past liaisons, who considered me an interloper. Glenn and I were the first of the band members to get married, which meant I had ended any chance for these women to continue past romances with him.

It was also hard because when we were on the road for a week or two there were no work prospects for me, and I started to flounder, not knowing what to do with myself. There was an unwritten agreement that I was a wife and should not be a member of the band.

I kept myself busy being a wife, confidant, and conspirator for the bandmates who were constantly breaking girls' hearts.

I was at the top of my game when I left Canada, but now, after three years on the road, I was disillusioned, filled with self-doubt and regret, and I began to question my decision to walk away from a very lucrative career.

There had been an early promise of settling down in Las Vegas, but for the first three years of marriage there was little opportunity to place roots anywhere. We were only in Las Vegas four months out of the year and when we were there, the drummer in the band and the random showgirl stayed at the house so it was hardly a home.

In the first year of marriage I fled to Hollywood and hit the town with Jean, but she was now engaged to Rich Little and had put her own career on hold to travel with him.

I reluctantly accepted the odd modeling job back in Canada, which meant leaving Glenn with an adoring fan base. After watching the way women threw themselves at the band, I wasn't sure that was a good idea. In time, I found a way to stay on the road and feel fulfilled by volunteering for charitable causes in every town.

CHAPTER SEVENTEEN

LAS VEGAS

*Las Vegas in the '60s and '70s was an exciting place
to call home.*

After spending several years circumnavigating the U.S. and
Canada, we found ourselves living in Las Vegas full time when
Glenn landed a permanent job in the Frontier Hotel's popular
Cloud Nine Lounge. We had a three-bedroom apartment near
the Strip that we shared, while we set our sights on one day
owning a home in our adopted city.

Las Vegas in the '60s and '70s was an exciting place. We
enjoyed the bright lights, the two-dollar shrimp cocktails,
the all-night buffets, and our celebrity and mafia connections. Want a comp show? Call Angelo at Caesars. Want
good seats, dinner, and a show in the Sands Copa Room?
Call Phil or Laura.

Las Vegas was like no other city. A unique aspect was hearing coins drop and bells ring at the slot machines that lined the walls at the entry and exit of every grocery store. You might bump into celebrities squeezing the grapefruit alongside you. If you were a late-night shopper, you would find a store full of showgirls after work buying food to feed their families, just like other mothers. Favorite amongst the shoppers at my local Safeway was Liberace, whose driver waited outside in a parked limo, while he browsed the aisles with his delightful countenance, greeting all whom he encountered.

While appearing in Toronto, Liberace (Lee to his friends), became involved with the "Famous People Players," a Canadian black-light-theater group. All the performers were disabled, and Lee featured them in his shows in Canada and Las Vegas.

Lee, who lived in an unassuming community around the corner from our home, would invite us over for small gatherings. He purchased the tract home in the same development as we did because it was less than a mile from the Strip. In the ensuing years, he added the property behind and next to him, encircled them with an elaborately-designed wrought iron fence festooned with his moniker, and installed his mother inside the compound.

As traveling entertainers, we carefully considered bringing a child into the world. Adding a much planned baby to the mix would force us to put down roots and round out our family. We looked forward to a more normal lifestyle and a better quality of life. Our child, of course, would be very talented and would one day come into the family business! After three years of marriage we found out we were about to become a trio.

As a pregnant mom, I dutifully paid careful attention to my food intake—fries were not on the menu—and when on occasion I found myself chomping down on an extra-large burger with all the fixings or a big milk chocolate bar, I would apologize to my little one and promise to do better. Thankfully, smoking and drinking were never part of my life.

In my third month, I experienced some spasms, which caused me great concern, but the doctor said we were healthy, and I'd be meeting my baby in six short months.

On comparing my growing tummy with those of the few expectant moms I came in contact with in my third trimester, I saw that I had not experienced the excessive weight gain they did—just good, healthy growth. My baby was peaceful and happy, and did very little shifting and kicking in my tummy. Just once or twice I saw a little foot sticking out the right side of my belly after a raucous rendition of Glenn's "Bumble Boogie" on the piano.

Although we moved from town to town and hotel to hotel with limited healthy food options, I sailed through my pregnancy. My doctor visits were happenstance and scattered, and each one led to a different due date. One thing the doctors agreed on was that it was a healthy pregnancy.

Little did I know that the birth of my child would dramatically alter my life forever. I had dug myself out of a miserable childhood, then spent years living the glamourous life of an entertainer. What was coming next was nothing I could have prepared for—and nothing I would have at first wished for.

CHAPTER EIGHTEEN

THE JUNKET FLIGHT

So, here's the thing. This was not your everyday junket flight.

I was eight months pregnant, sitting excitedly in a window seat on the tarmac of the Las Vegas executive terminal waiting for takeoff. Plans had been made, careful preparations were in the works, the future was ahead, and I was in control.

The journey to Toronto, Canada took place on a junket flight packed with people enthusiastically sharing stories of monies lost and gained on the gambling tables; the many shows and buffets partaken of; the alcohol consumed; and the sins committed. The hilarity was still palpable with little accountability for actions left behind in the desert heat. Respectability would return on the ride home; but for now, it was still party time aboard the aircraft.

Flight attendants busily tended to pre-flight business closing overhead luggage compartments, taking drink orders from the first-class cabin, and readying for a five-hour flight.

The pilots were going through their routine checks as we sat on the runway on a hot Las Vegas day. Inside the plane, the air, or rather the lack of it was stifling. Passengers were sweating as they chattered with each other, fanning their faces with in-flight magazines.

I was excited to get going, and more than ready to face a new future that included our much-anticipated baby. In 1970, aviation laws allowed near-term expectant mothers to travel at their own risk. My doctor had written an "all clear to travel" note in the event I was turned away, and with a month to go, I wasn't worried.

I was concerned, however, that the lack of air in the packed cabin, made worse by the horrible cigarette smoke that permeated the entire plane, would cause me to get motion sick, which I was prone to. I never wanted to be as sick as I was when I was ten and I traveled by ship from England to Canada.

Cigarettes and cigars were allowed on flights in those days. Although smokers were typically confined to the last fifteen rows, the rules on junkets were relaxed. On this Air Canada Flight 73, it seemed like all 250 passengers were puffing away.

As we started down the runway, it felt like I was on the verge of an anxiety attack. I wasn't sure I could hold onto my breakfast as I tried to calm myself.

Count to one hundred. It's only four and a half hours to Toronto. Eat the saltines slowly; focus on the journey ahead and take long, deep breaths. In through the mouth, out through the nose...or was it the reverse?

I finally heard the full-throttle of the engines as the wheels went up. We were on our way. I'd had butterflies last night and this morning, realizing I was embarking on an exciting life that would include a baby. I considered all the diverse and interesting friends we had made over the years who would be in our child's life and I began to relax.

I remembered the celebration the night before when Elvis Presley and his entourage came to see Glenn perform alongside the legendary Fats Domino in the Driftwood Lounge at the Flamingo Hotel.

People in the hotel went wild as Elvis, that's right, not an impersonator, no, the real Elvis of "Blue Suede Shoes" and Priscilla fame, entered the building. Instantly, the lounge was packed to capacity.

Wayne was also appearing at the Flamingo Hotel, but "Mr. Las Vegas" was performing in the main showroom.

The junket flight

Upon hearing that Elvis was in the house, he joined the after-show festivities backstage. It was an amazing night, and I was dazzled to be in the company of such celebrity icons.

Glenn met Elvis a few years earlier when Glenn was getting standing ovations as the opening act for Wayne Newton at the Frontier Hotel. One night, Elvis came backstage after the show to see Wayne. While there, he offered Glenn a job with his band. Glenn and I talked it over, and as unbelievable as it sounded, we agreed he should politely decline the offer.

By joining the band and going on the road with Elvis, Glenn would have faded into the background. He was the front man in his own successful touring show, and his career was taking off with appearances on national TV shows and the opening act for people like Wayne, Gladys Knight, and Bill Cosby.

Glenn resolved not to just be a face in the crowd on stage. Instead, he would continue his independent path and hope for stardom one day. Nonetheless, Elvis and Glenn became friends and Glenn enjoyed hanging out with the band backstage at the Las Vegas Hilton.

I was obviously in the final stages of impending motherhood, and last night many famous people placed their hands on my protruding belly. I was assured it was a good luck gesture that ensured a healthy baby.

Glenn also secured Elvis's autograph for his brother, which I was to take to Toronto. This famous signature was not given without an embarrassing moment for both Glenn and me.

We knew Elvis was coming backstage after the show, and months prior, Glenn's younger brother had begged him to get an autograph if we ever saw Elvis again. We knew it wasn't cool for one assumed peer to impose on another, but Glenn wanted to please his brother and eventually got up the nerve.

He waited for the right moment when Elvis was settled in and relaxed. Then he sauntered over and launched into the appeal.

"Elvis," Glenn said, "My kid brother is a big fan of yours as we all are, and it would mean so much to him if he could get your autograph. Linda is flying to Toronto in the morning and she will take it to him. So can I have your Elvagraph. Auto?"

As this faux pas hung in the air, we wanted to be swallowed up and disappear. Elvis considered the so not cool "Elvagraph" request for a moment. Then he and his entourage fell on the floor laughing while our faces turned beet red.

In his inimitable drawl, he asked, "Should I sign it Elvis or Auto?" This followed with more peals of laughter. He knew that Glenn was mortified by his request and slapped him on the back and signed it with great humor, kindness, and a flourish. He handed this little piece of gold to me, and I tucked it away as Glenn looked sheepishly on.

Through our gaming connections, we were delighted to have secured a free nonstop junket flight for me from Las Vegas directly to Toronto this morning. Glenn saw me off at the airport, and vowed to join me as soon as he finished his contract in a few days, while I made arrangements for an obstetrician and hospital to deliver our baby in a month.

Glenn's next gig was in the highly respected and coveted Imperial Room at the world-renowned Royal York Hotel. Entertainers who had performed at the nightclub included luminaries like Marlene Dietrich, Tony Bennett, Peggy Lee, Ray Charles, and Tina Turner. Glenn Smith was about to join that esteemed list.

We hoped our baby would be born during that time. Otherwise, we would be at the next gig in Cleveland, Ohio with little time to find a local doctor.

After the flight took off, I did my best to relax, which was hard considering I was squished into a window seat with a tummy that allowed little room to put the seat-back tray down and made using a seat belt difficult. The two ladies sitting next to me in the middle and aisle seats were smoking and talking about their last night in Las Vegas, while I thought about how Glenn's booking at the Imperial Room would be a game changer for his career.

Suddenly my thoughts were interrupted by a spasm that shot through my bloated body.

What was that? Woah! That's not supposed to happen, not now. What is that dull ache and why is my tummy hurting now of all times? Is it indigestion? Oooh, cripes. . . There it is again.

I tried to find a more comfortable position in the cramped space, but a dull ache in my lower back and abdomen made the journey very uncomfortable. The ladies next to me were conscious of my squirming, so to put them at ease I told then a lame joke about a pregnant lady, an Irishman, and a rabbi. They didn't laugh. Embarrassed, I started humming the Bee Gees song, "I Started a Joke."

But no matter what I did, the ache was still there. On top of that, a few jabs from my baby's foot made me more uncomfortable with each passing minute. And the flight had just begun.

Noooooo, calm down. . . Take slow deep breaths and focus on the large bald head of the man in the seat in front of me. Ahhhh, that's much better.

A little while later the pain started again, only this time it was intense. I tried my best to deal with it, but eventually I levitated out of my seat and let out a loud whimper.

My concerned seatmates turned and asked me when my due date was, but my body language and the look on my face let them know in no uncertain terms that I was not in the mood for conversation, and they left me alone.

I was miserable. I tried to stand up and make my way to the aisle to no avail. My seatmates were becoming very concerned, and cool cloths and fans materialized.

Then others around me also became concerned, and they began fretting and fawning over me offering me beverages, crackers, nuts, and various other items.

For as long as I could recall, when dealing with a detractor, I could hold my feelings in check and strategize a beneficial outcome. I was at my best after a quick kick to the curb. This was a learned habit after fighting my way up from the morass of my early childhood. I would willingly go for the throat when an innocent person was hurt or maligned. But when kindness or a sympathetic gesture was directed my way, I choked up and tears started to flow.

The sympathy of the cabin crew and the passengers were too much for me to handle. What little air flowed through the cabin had been sucked out by an unseen force, and it felt like I was suffocating. That coupled with the rings of smoke circling my head, the intense, awful smell of cigars from the back of the plane, the sweat from so many people, and the jam-packed space, caused my stomach to lurch.

Someone please tell my seatmates to stop fawning and blowing smoke in my face. And *please tell these increasingly painful contractions to stop.*

I started having a full-on panic attack wondering if this baby was really coming, or if my typical nausea was worse due to the confined, stuffy space.

And then I was suddenly as sick as I had ever been with great heaving gyrations and projectile vomiting. Paper bags were passed up and down the aisle from everyone's seat pocket. My retching, which could be heard throughout the plane, was certain to be causing great distress for some flyers.

The flight attendants, who had been busy with their many in-flight duties, were becoming more alarmed as there seemed to be no end to my vomiting. Concerned, they asked if I was in labor. In a stupid and futile attempt to reassure them I said, "I don't think so."

Between gritted teeth and gut-wrenching spewing, I told them I was prone to motion sickness and sometimes it was worse than others. After an hour of vomiting, the dry heaving started, accompanied by major stomach contractions. As expected, word went around the cabin that a delusional, sick, pregnant lady was about to give birth on the plane.

Fortunately, it wasn't your typical junket flight.

Junket flights began in the 1950s to entice players to come to Las Vegas to gamble. Casino operators would hire junket reps to fill a plane with qualified gamblers. These players would get free airfare, hotel accommodations, meals, shows (and just about anything else they wanted) in exchange for their commitment to gamble a specific number of hours per day at an explicit average amount. The casinos were gambling that the players would lose more than their out-of-pocket expenses for flying, housing, feeding, and entertaining them. These flights were often offered to industries with many high-end executives, and my flight was no exception.

Unbelievably, this junket was comprised of two hundred half-inebriated, exhausted doctors and nurses: Surely there was an obstetrician or two on board. Whatever was going on with me, I was in capable hands.

An hour into the flight it became apparent to all on board that I was in full-blown labor. Apparent, that is, to everyone but me. This was my first baby, and I was clueless and in denial. I had not taken any typical expectant parenting classes due in part to a traveling schedule crisscrossing the country from nightclub to nightclub. I was in this on my own and uninformed.

I had no idea that this pain was not the result of losing my cookies until there was nothing left in my system to spew. But two-hundred plus medical attendants assured me this was the real deal.

"Lady, you're in labor, and we are here to help," someone said.

I later heard that having just left Sin City, everyone on board was placing bets on when I would deliver, how much the baby would weight, what the sex would be, and who would do the honors and deliver this kid mid-flight.

Everything was a blur as hands lifted me, and many concerned faces came and went. And then the captain himself stopped by the makeshift bed. . . or was that Ernest Borgnine of *McHale's Navy* fame, dressed in captain's attire?

My head was swimming. . .

However ludicrous, it appeared that this famous guy was beaming down at me, a gap-tooth smile reminiscent of his days on a deserted island.

It soon occurred to me that at some point in the drama, I had been extracted from my coach seat and moved into the first-class cabin, where two rows of passengers were standing to give me room to plop my baby out. It was crowded and hot, and many people were involved when Captain Ernest Borgnine asked me if I was planning on giving birth right now on his flight.

He, like all the others, was asking about the severity of the contractions and the length of time between them, and whether I felt I would soon give birth.

Shaking my head I convinced him and myself that this was just a bad case of motion sickness. He said if I could hold on, he would continue to Pearson Airport in Toronto, otherwise, with a nod from me, he would land in Chicago.

I was fast becoming delirious, but I could tell that the captain wanted me to give him the thumbs up for the plane to keep going. He said conspiratorially with a wink and an attempt at seriousness that made me want to cross my legs and hold on for dear life that If he remained on course to Toronto, his wife would be so very happy because he would be home in time for dinner for a change, and I would be the hysterical heroine of an unfolding comedy show.

Of course I wanted to please him.

In hushed tones, the captain extracted an agreement from me to continue into Canadian airspace. He spoke softly, pointing out that with an emergency on board, he would be sure to get clearance to land ahead of all other flights. Additionally, he assured me he had delivered a baby on a plane once before.

It never occurred to me to ask him who was flying the plane now, or why, for God's sake, Ernest Borgnine was the pilot of this plane? And if in fact he was the pilot, who would land the plane if he was in the middle of delivering a baby? He said it was up to me. . . either way an emergency landing was called for. There would be a waiting ambulance at whichever airport I chose.

And so, I found myself under the worst circumstances faced with the biggest decision of my life that would ultimately have consequences and ramifications far greater than I could ever have anticipated or imagined.

Chicago spelled out problems for sure. I would be alone in a city with no family or friends, giving birth to a baby with no one to proudly show him off to.

On the off-chance Glenn could arrive in time for the delivery, it would be for a quick "Hello, baby" and then a plane back to work. That would be expensive. And there would be even more expense because I would have to take another flight to Toronto with a newborn baby and whatever gear was necessary.

We had made the hasty decision to fly to Toronto on this junket flight because it was free. It made sense because I was only eight months pregnant, and I would have time to shop for things for the baby while Glenn made the rounds to promote his appearance there. Neither one of us had entertained the thought that I would have the baby mid-flight.

And now here I was delirious and in between bouts of pain, I had to decide whether to have the baby in Chicago or Toronto. And I had to decide quickly.

I couldn't help but feel a sense of responsibility to the plane load of Canadians who were anxious to get home. There were certain to be loved ones waiting for them at the airport, and I didn't want to be the reason they were inconvenienced.

So when the captain quietly said, "It's your call. . . Do you want to continue to Toronto or land in the Windy City, I said between gasps, *"Please take me home to Toronto where family from both sides will be waiting to greet this newest addition."*

Despite advanced labor, I made it to Toronto with a plane full of doctors and nurses cheering me on. As the plane landed, we could see on the tarmac an ambulance racing toward us with sirens wailing and lights signaling. An emergency descent had been authorized and onto the plane came an assortment of paramedics and cops. It must have been a slow news day, as I also noticed a camera crew.

There was lots of whooping and hollering, well-wishing and cheering as the paramedics checked my vitals and strapped me onto the gurney.

As they ferried me off the plane to the ambulance, I passed by a phalanx of hands, all patting me on the head and tummy.

When my erstwhile hero, Captain Borgnine said goodbye, he made it clear to me that there was much disappointment emanating from every corner of the plane because I was being carted off to North York General Hospital rather than having the baby onboard and everyone had lost their bets. Nevertheless, I bravely waved goodbye to my fellow passengers and received another raucous cheer.

CHAPTER NINETEEN

MAY 15, 1970

*Would he have extraordinary musical talent and
be a child prodigy like his dad, who could play piano
and flute at three?*

The ambulance careened around corners as it made its way to North York General, the nearest hospital to the Toronto airport, while the paramedics checked my vitals and marveled that I had traveled all the way from Las Vegas to plunk my baby down in their great city.

I arrived on a stretcher late in the afternoon, and my precious son was born a few minutes before midnight as I held on for dear life, not wanting to expel my child into the arms of strangers. It was a five-ticket ride, and I was on it to the end.

Now I was in a large stark hospital room with gleaming white paint on the walls, a few floral bouquets and a lonely teddy bear sitting at attention on the window pane.

A red maple tree bearing drooping clusters of small, smoky red flowers tapped at the window, willing me to wake up and greet the beautiful spring day.

As I drifted in and out of coherent thought, I noticed through half-closed eyes, that a male orderly was quietly and efficiently pushing moms in their beds out of the unadorned, antiseptic hospital room. In my groggy mental state, he seemed to be doing this task in slow motion.

My son was born Canadian to a British mom and a Canadian dad, who were residents of the United States.

There would be so many travel options for him.

Noting his date of birth, May 15, 1970, inscribed on the hospital room's chalkboard alongside the names of the delivering doctor and charge nurse, I marveled at all that had transpired in the past twenty-four hours. It was just one full day since I left a backstage party with Elvis at the Flamingo Hotel in Las Vegas to board a Boeing 727 bound for Toronto.

What stories I would have to tell.

I was exhausted from the ordeal. It had been a long hard labor rife with vomitus maximus on a jet plane, intense lower back pain for more hours than I cared to count, and now, an all-consuming aloneness in a country that was no longer home. I was sapped both physically and emotionally, but anxious to hold my new baby in my arms. I knew I would be the best, most loving mom ever.

As the orderly cast his eyes about in a final sweep of the room, he gathered up the flowers and the little stuffed bear belonging to my departing roommates, leaving me alone.

While all this activity was transpiring, a reed-thin nurse with pursed lips scurried about, adjusting my bed and fussing over the large and glorious bouquet of congratulatory flowers delivered to me last night. The aromatic scent of this magnificent arrangement of jasmine and roses had heralded its arrival. The card was signed, "Well wishes from Fats Domino."

I had briefly spoken to Glenn two hours after giving birth, telling him about the harrowing plane ride, the sirens, the two hundred medical experts on board, and my decision not to land in Chicago but to soldier on to Toronto instead. He was shocked and relieved at the same time. Excitedly I told him that we were the parents of a gorgeous, healthy, seven pound baby boy, whom I couldn't wait to hold. Thrilled, he passed the phone around, and I glowed as I received congratulatory messages from the band, the staff, and celebrity friends.

The hospital staff took note of the celebrities on the other end as I mentioned names like Wayne Newton, Fats Domino, and even Elvis, conveying that I had friends in high places.

But today, given the recent rearrangement of beds and the comings and goings of hospital staff, it appeared that something of great importance was about to take place very soon in this room. It was tense in my little corner of the world, and though I was puzzled about this sudden flurry of activity, I was at the same time sad to see my three roommates leave. They had been quite entertaining while I waited for my baby to be brought to me.

Mommy number one was very pretty and didn't look like she had just given birth, despite her red nose and puffy eyes. Her hair was shining and groomed and she wore a beautiful shawl resplendent with a delicately woven floral ensemble. Before she vacated the room, she had been visited by a large group of concerned family members; and her young husband, whose face was colorless, paced the room as if he was shell-shocked.

What on earth was going on?

I tried not to stare as I quietly observed them, speculating whether their baby had been stillborn or was critically ill. Considerable wails had emanated from bed number one for quite some time and it was unsettling. I was concerned for this young mom who was about my age, who had to deal with a yet unnamed catastrophe. I resolved to ask my roomie what had upset her so much once her family left.

Watching from my corner of the large room, Mommy One's beautiful, swaddled baby had been wheeled into the room with plenty of oohs and ahhs going on as the family marveled at this perfect child. But there was still a lot of consoling going on, and I was mystified. Eventually the congregation around the bed bid their leave and gave Daddy several encouraging hugs and arm squeezes.

Eventually I learned that I had mistakenly assumed there was a problem regarding the birth of the baby. The reason Mommy One had cried all night and all morning, was because she wanted a boy, and instead she had given birth to a baby girl. She recently had the nursery painted blue and because of her certainty of the baby's sex, all the gifts came in hues of blue, which resulted in her resorting to giant gulping sobs and all manner of blame. . .mostly directed at her sweet and helpless husband, who looked on miserably. It was obvious there were big problems in that family.

Mommy number two was quite the spectacle—rumpled and belligerent, big red hair wildly dispersed in many directions, bright red lipstick on her ample mouth and teeth, and a deep, penetrating, commanding voice.

Mommy Two who I affectionately called "Big Red" made all kinds of demands that annoyed the staff and me. First, she barked orders to the nurses to bring her dinner NOW, then more pillows to prop up her great frame. "Bring me magazines, more food. . . I am famished. You can't expect me to eat this hospital crap." She juggled her newest baby, the phone, a milkshake, and several kidlets, who bounced on her bed demanding to eat her leftover pudding and the chocolates that lay on her lap.

All day, with triumphant eyes, she announced to everyone who crossed her path and to those within earshot, that "This is my fifth and last baby. My tubes are now tied, and I have finally put a stop to the baby-breeding business."

Mommy number three was me.

I was, in my own estimation, an expert in the baby delivery business, given my recent dramatic arrival from the airport with sirens blaring. I had successfully delivered a sweet baby boy after ten hours of labor while traversing two countries. It was by this logic alone that I judged "Mommy Number One" and "Mommy Number Two" as inadequate and undeserving of their recently delivered bundles of humanity. I was the best mom in the room and I couldn't wait to prove it.

Where was my little guy anyway?

It didn't matter to me if my child was a boy or a girl, if he had blue eyes or brown, or was wrinkled and scrawny with no hair, if he weighed five pounds or ten, or had freckles like mine.

Of course, I wanted him to have the correct number of fingers and toes, but most of all I simply wanted a healthy baby. I wanted to hold him in my arms and love him forever and let him know that he was the luckiest little boy on the planet because I was his mom, and together we would conquer the world.

As I lay waiting for the baby to be brought to me, Glenn was 3,000 miles away performing at the Flamingo Hotel. I pictured him with his band and friends celebrating on the Las Vegas Strip. This was the first grandchild on either side of our families, and being a boy was sure to make his grandparents happy and proud.

I thought how lucky he was to be our son. We had mulled over and discussed many options before deciding on his name. He would be our beloved Christopher.

Would he have extraordinary musical talent and be a child prodigy like his dad, who could play piano and flute at three? Or would he be a fighter like his mom, overcoming all obstacles in his way, battling his way to the top, and kicking all detractors to the curb?

God knows I had my share of challenges, and I wanted our child to be book smart because I certainly wasn't.

I imagined reading to him every single day, and by age two he would recognize no fewer than two hundred words, maybe more. He would identify each word by pointing at the object. He would climb up on my lap and ask for "More stories, Mommy," and then recite them back to me. People would envy how intelligent this amazing child was.

Had I slept some more?
Where did they take the other moms?
Where was my baby?

Perhaps they were waiting to wheel me out too.
Was someone more important in need of this room?
Where was I going?
What was going to happen next?

I was alone now in the cold and austere room, and I fully expected a marching band to troop in.

Eventually the delivery-room doctor came in with his staff. He looked awkward in his doctor's garb, as though loaned a costume that didn't match his persona. He was tall with jet black hair and a stooped and gaunt body that appeared to be carrying the weight of the world on his too-thin frame.

He looked somewhat familiar. I had a mild recollection of his coming into the delivery room last night at the command of the brusque Scottish nurse who attended to me in the labor room when it appeared that this baby had no intention of coming into the world.

My baby would take its own time, thank you very much.

She had been unpleasant and inconsiderate of my predicament at the time. After all I had come to the hospital in an ambulance as an emergency case, and I was totally alone. As I twisted and turned and the contractions got longer, stronger, and closer together, I had longed for a compassionate face, and some words of kindness and encouragement. I had spent hours in labor freaking out, and Nurse Ratchet had held off offering me any kind of relief for the excruciating pain I was going through.

Now the doctor, flanked by two expressionless nurses, stood as still as a frightened cat at the head of my bed, silently appraising me as though I was in a petri dish. He looked at me with probing eyes the color of coal, then he coughed and quickly glanced around the room.

His demeanor was unnerving, and I felt my heart flutter. *Why was he so grim? He must be having a bad day.*

Eventually he introduced himself, and asked in cold, matter-of-fact way, a question that will be forever seared onto the frontal lobe of my brain.

CHAPTER TWENTY

ABNORMALITY

RETARDATION?

His question echoed in the empty room, bouncing off the walls, vibrating, pulsing.

"Do you know anything about mental retardation?"

WHAT. . .?

Blank, bewildered, startled, I stared at his mouth and stammered, "I. . .I. . .don't understand what you said. . .Could you repeat that?"

"A chromosome mutation, a structural abnormality in one or more chromosomes. Trisomy 21. It's the presence of three chromosomes rather than the usual two matched pair of chromosomes. Trisomy 21 is also known as Down syndrome."

WHAT...?

An alarm went off. *WHAT HAD I DONE?*

In any setting, when something of great importance is about to happen, the silence is deafening. The sounds in the room stilled. It was my turn to speak and no words would form.

What on earth were they saying?

Was I dreaming?

What abnormality?

The words hung in the air . . . *did I hear what I thought I heard? Did he say mutation of chromosomes? Something to do with DNA? Abnormal. . . abnormalities. . . RETARDATION?*

Those were terrifying words that nothing could have prepared me for.

Seeing and hearing nothing from me other than an open mouth and blank stare, the doctor tackled the question once more, blinking several times.

"Have you heard the term Down syndrome? It's more commonly referred to as mongolism."

WHAT? Please don't say that.

One of the nurses started to cluck, rolling her eyes, giving the doctor a withering look. The other's eyes bored right through me, expressionless.

He eventually continued in his quest to destroy my life.

"I am sorry to tell you that your baby is profoundly disabled. He has mental retardation and a whole host of medical issues."

I looked uncomprehendingly at him, imploring his cohorts to stop him from uttering those terrible words. My eyes cast about as I struggled to absorb the relevance of his statement. I was a dancer. I was healthy. I never smoked or drank. I ate right and exercised. I had a great pregnancy. My baby was happy and relaxed in my belly for the entire pregnancy. No complaints from him.

Mongoloid?

This word was frightening, loathsome. It conjured up images of alien beings.

Why is he saying this stupid, hurtful thing?

Shut up and go away. . .

Is this a dream?

The clicking fan overhead seemed to be short-circuiting, moving in slow motion. *Click, spin, click, spin,* as the doctor swayed and shifted from foot to foot, peering at me from under bushy eyebrows. I started to hyperventilate. Gasping for breath, I silently screamed, while awaiting the next awful pronouncement.

Why won't he stand still?

He launched into the next statement, matter-of-factly continuing on. "In addition to the issues with his retardation. . .his chromosome abnormality—"

Abnormality

DAMN. He said it again.

"Your baby has many problems, including a serious heart defect. He has respiratory problems and other related issues. His health is extremely compromised."

This last comment rushed through as though he couldn't get the words out fast enough.

"The good news is that we don't expect him to survive."

As the words slipped and slurred from his mouth, bile formed in my stomach promising to become an explosive propelling charge that would send them running.

I felt myself slowly suffocating. A trap had been set, and the noose was tightening, cutting off the remaining breath from my lungs. I was cornered. . .a trapped rat, an evil person, a prisoner with the most serious of offenses being read out loud. A death sentence. The death of dreams.

Gulping and blinking, I gasped for air. The standing trio looked like they wanted to immediately take flight and distance themselves from this horrific situation. I looked at each one, my eyes imploring their help. It wasn't forthcoming. They were just the delivery folks. And then, a slight reprieve.

"We have checked your chromosomes, and there is nothing wrong with you. We suspect that when we check your husband, he will be fine, too."

The doctor smiled slightly, the modulation of his words intended to reassure a bewildered patient. It was exceedingly clear to him that I understood precious little of what was being said, that I was in a fog. It was certainly a dilemma for this man, imparting such news with just one-half of the responsible parents present.

Coughing, clearing his throat, he continued, "There are places for babies like this; you don't ever have to take him home. You can have another baby and forget about this one!"

He said this with a lift in his voice.

"Should you decide to take this baby home, which we don't advise you do, you should know you won't be accepted by society. You may as well live on Center Island."

What was he saying?
Why did he seem happier now?
Was he giving me permission to abandon this baby?

Center Island was a tiny hamlet, a few hundred yards off Lake Ontario, a twenty minute ferry ride from downtown Toronto Center. Originally the home of various native peoples, including the Ojibwa and Mississauga tribes, Center Island was now inhabited by fewer than three hundred full-time residents. The implication that moving there was the best course of action was the doctor's way of saying that I would be isolated by society for the rest of my life if I took this child home.

With all this talk about matters that were incomprehensible to me, of needing to move to a distant island, of dumping this child and his chromosome abnormalities, retardation, Mongolism, and more, I felt myself slipping away. The group at the end of my bed began to take on the appearance of characters in a play, straight out of central casting. A stethoscope hung importantly from the doctor's neck, while the nurses in starched white uniforms radiated efficiency as they stood ramrod still with downcast eyes.

He continued, "Prenatal screening reveals this problem, and most expectant mothers will abort these defective babies early in their pregnancy. However, one in every 2,200 live births still results in this situation. So you are not alone."

Did he just smile?

"Do you have any questions? We know this comes as a shock, that you will need time to process this information. We understand that your husband is in Las Vegas. Is there anyone we can call?"

*Yes. . .*I thought. *Call someone else. PLEASE, I don't want you in my room. Take those nurses with their disapproving smirks and get out of here—NOW.*

I was drowning. I tried to swim up, but was held down by some unknown force. Shame and regret permeated my thoughts. I must have done something bad to deserve this.

"The sins of your father," I whispered to myself. It was payback time.

Is this a disease that I caught? Is it contagious?

Is this why I am all alone in this room? Surely this isn't real.

And then the realization, the relief that this was a dream, just not a nice one.

The apparitions at the end of the bed slowly merged into an amorphous, shapeless, floating white cloud that faded from view. Thank God, I could control this awful dream. I could close my eyes, stop the pain, and wake up to an entirely new reality.

As a youngster I had dreams that left me gasping for breath. Vivid, frightening dreams of monsters taking me away in the night; dreams of falling down the steep, narrow stairs from my upstairs bedroom and never landing, just falling forever.

Those dreams of running through the woods away from the monsters at night or falling forever were terrifying. They stayed with me into adulthood until I realized I was no longer vulnerable to the actions of others. I was fearless.

Starting in my later teens after the deportation of my father, I had dreams of flying. Gathering all the momentum I could muster, I could leap up from a standing position, flap my arms, and gather enough energy and impetus to glide effortlessly. Not too high, just up there observing the world below. It was such a powerful feeling—I could look down and see my future self.

I continued to have those dreams as an adult, and if I found myself unable to take off, I attributed it to some inde-cisiveness in my life or work. Flying gave me the exhilarating feeling of freedom that I could defy gravity, that I was superwoman.

Dozing off once again in my hospital room, I dreamed of the circus. . . the best circus ever. Trapeze artists performed the most amazing feats. And I was there too—the tent was packed with adoring fans who watched me fly at breathtaking heights across the empty air and land on the high wire. A clown jumped onto the wire and beckoned me forward.

Really?

Then relief, as I danced across the high wire without a net below. I was that good. It was hysterically funny, and I laughed big gulping belly laughs.

The clown beckoned again. Then his funny face turned into my old nemesis, the monster of my childhood dreams and I fell. . . I fell for miles...I fell forever. . . until a hand reached out at the last minute and I pirouetted back to the relative safety of the perch. I was safe now, asleep, blessed sleep. Everything would be OK when I woke up from this nightmare.

The monsters at the end of the bed turned and quietly left the room.

The memory of what had happened didn't kick in until I fully resurfaced from a drugged sleep. I experienced a heightened electrical activation in my brain, a moment where I surveyed the room and then, slowly felt the horror, an awakening accompanied by heartache like I'd never known before. This was not a nightmare, this was real.

I wanted to escape the grief and go back to sleep and never wake up. I wanted to go back into a fantasy world and dream. I wanted to be comatose again. But it was not to be.

CHAPTER TWENTY-ONE

THE DAY AFTER

He looked a bit like me, a bit like his dad, and a bit like our Chinese neighbors.

Hot tears spilled down my face, and feelings of guilt permeated my thoughts as I bargained with God,

"Please, if you can do me this one favor, if you can change this in some way, make this a dream, make the doctors wrong, or, at the very least, heal this baby. I promise I will be a better person. I won't eat junk food. I will be nicer to my friends. I will dedicate my life to doing good work in the world."

But God was having none of it.

I wondered what we would say to friends, to strangers when asked if we had kids. To all the people who saw me pregnant, and all Glenn's fans? Why did this have to happen to me? Glenn and I were both healthy. Show business friends were getting high from every type of substance, while I wouldn't even take an aspirin.

But it didn't matter how healthy I was. Chris's condition was caused by an extra chromosome sneaking in at conception. How random is that? What causes an extra chromosome to sneak in anyway? Trisomy 21 is the technical term. Trisomy is genetic, but it's rarely passed down from parent to child. Trisomy is like many cancers, a random mistake.

A number of mistakes can happen in a cell to cause cancer; a very specific mistake happens when an egg gets made. My son was a mistake.

In the end, it all came down to balance. If your DNA is like a recipe of "you," then every gene is an ingredient. If you throw in too much of an ingredient (like an extra chromosome), you mess up the entire recipe. Extra chromosomes can cause miscarriages, and I thought back to those first few months when I had spasms and it felt like I was going to lose the baby. The doctor had been right: My baby was stubborn. He had held on for dear life. He wasn't going to leave my cozy body.

Considering this child's tenacity, I wanted to march into the nursery and pluck the extra chromosome out of every one of his cells and fix him. My moods fluctuated from anger to sorrow to fear to pity, all directed at selfish me. Then I was filled with an all-consuming guilt.

I must have done something to cause this. Did I travel too much? Could I have seen the signs sooner and been more prepared? What should I have been looking for? And what difference would it have made anyway?

My son had Down syndrome, which meant that if he did in fact survive, he would be developmentally delayed forever. This was an unfixable condition. That night, I read a leaflet that had been placed beside my bed:

Birth Defect: Abnormalities of structure, function, or body metabolism present at birth. Major defects are abnormalities that lead to developmental or physical disabilities.
Disability means: Having a physical or mental health condition or a health problem that restricts the ability to engage in activities of daily living.

According to the U.S. Centers for Disease Control and Prevention, about one in thirty-three babies is born with a birth defect. Birth defects can be caused by genetic, environmental, or unknown factors. Most babies with birth defects are born to two parents with no health problems or risk factors. . . .

The day after

For a list of birth defects refer to. . .
For advice to prevent birth defects refer to. . .

Down syndrome was named for Langdon Down in 1866. He referred to his subjects as Mongoloids or Mongoloid idiots on the basis that their faces, with slightly slanted eyes, resembled those of people from Mongolia. Doctor Down proposed that human evolution had gone from black people to Asians to white people, and that white people born with Mongolism were a throwback to their primitive Asian ancestors.

E. Samuel G. Howe's 1848 report to the Massachusetts legislature articulated this eugenic, dehumanizing vision: "This class of persons is always a burden upon the public. Persons of this class are idle and often mischievous and are dead weights upon the material prosperity of the state. They are even worse than useless. Every such person is like an Upas tree that poisons the whole moral atmosphere about him."

Glenn's family arrived at the hospital that morning. When told of the baby's condition in the hallway, my father-in-law keeled over and needed medical attention. They never made it to my room. This was the first grandchild, and there had been such hope.

Jean was made of different stuff.

Upon hearing of my admittance to the hospital, Jean, who was appearing in a musical in downtown Toronto, rushed to the hospital, where she found me sleeping. A tight-lipped nurse suggested she leave and come back tomorrow. They didn't know Jean.

Before long she managed to extract news of the baby and the circumstances of his birth. Sometime later, I heard that

Jean caused a commotion in the hospital, demanding to see the doctor who had given her sister such bad news. It was clear to her on meeting Christopher that they had to be wrong.

There for the long haul, she sat by my bed until I awoke from yet another drug-induced stupor and saw her sweet face. I also saw the sadness and concern in her eyes before she wiped away the tears and smiled bravely.

She hugged me tight, and with unspoken words conveyed her heartache. She and I shared a bond that came from both of us having experienced the pain and heartache that no one should have to go through. We had fought our way through the abuse and ensuing chaos, and had achieved a measure of success in our lives.

Although heartbroken for me and the baby, Jean was enchanted when she saw him in the incubator looking so tiny, vulnerable and defenseless. She became an advocate for this little helpless child, saying how utterly beautiful he was. She said he was an angel, not the creature that I had recently been told to imagine.

She said, "He is special, a gift. This little guy needs you to be strong for the short time he has on earth. Go now and break the news to Glenn and help him adjust. I will stay here around the clock, keep an eye on the baby, and keep you updated on his condition. Then you can drive back to Toronto together as quickly as you can. You should be back in three days; it's the best thing to do. You can't give Glenn this awful news over the phone."

Jean knew Glenn well. He was a child prodigy, and his musical abilities had paved the way for a life of adulation and ease. He had been protected for most of his life and adored by his family and friends. He had grown up in a supportive and loving, blissfully normal family with a working dad and a stay-at-home mom, where dinner was on the table each night precisely at five o'clock. Glenn could not be alone when he heard this devastating news. I had to be by his side.

The day after

It also made sense because a week from now Glenn was scheduled to open in Toronto at one of the most important venues of his career. He would have to drive the car with a trailer hitched to it filled with the band's musical equipment several thousand miles. I knew it would be too dangerous to let my husband, who would be grief-stricken after hearing the devastating news about our son, drive alone for three days. I was not prepared to lose Glenn as well as my child.

And so, In the middle of the night, Jean called our mother and elicited her help in watching over the baby while I flew to Las Vegas.

By now Jean was again living in Toronto. After six years with Universal Studios, playing parts in *Planet of the Apes*, *Star*, and *Space Odyssey*, she had become disenchanted with life in L.A. She had broken off the engagement to Rich Little and was now a nightclub singer and actress.

My father had ruined Jean's life, and she could not put her tragic childhood behind her. Low self-esteem and feelings of unworthiness caused her to constantly run, engage in self-destructive behavior, and sabotage her success every chance she got.

After Rich Little, Jean dated the actor Alan Thicke and then Alan Hamel, who would later marry Suzanne Somers. She drove a Bentley and bought a ranch and a farm, and lost it all. If she made money, she gave it away. She was a lost soul who was always changing religions, looking for answers that were never forthcoming.

The roles had reversed, and I was now helping my sister and my mother, who lived together in the home Glenn and I had purchased in the Rosedale section of Toronto. I would provide for my mother for the rest of her life. But today I needed them, and they both came running.

It seemed like an easy decision to make. I should leave right away. And yet I was filled with the nagging thought that I was abandoning my son.

In the meantime, Jean called around for available direct flights to Las Vegas, which I had just left twenty-four hours ago. She and my mom would stay at the hospital to field phone calls from anxious family members and keep a crib-side vigil.

Jean spent considerable time consoling and chastising me as I waivered in my decision to fly to Las Vegas.

You can't wait for Glenn to drive all the way to Toronto before you tell him. He will never forgive you. Do you see anyone in his family offering to fly there and deliver the news and accompany him back here? Linda, they are devastated. You are strong; you have always made lemonade out of lemons. I know it's a bitter pill to swallow, but it's you who should go. The baby is in good hands here, and you can call me every few hours to check on him.

I managed to avoid all the incoming phone calls, and the staff helped by explaining that I had experienced a difficult birth and was sleeping.

After sorting out a course of action for the next few hours and the ensuing days, we agreed that I would fly to Las Vegas, I would tell Glenn, and we would drive back to Toronto together. In the meantime Jean would be the baby's advocate until we returned. My hope was that Glenn and I would figure out a way to cope with a future without the perfect, healthy baby we had wanted so much.

It had now been more than twenty-four hours since I had given birth, and I had yet to see my baby, who was so critically ill. I was not calling him Christopher. That name had been reserved for another boy, a perfect little boy, one with a future, not one that was doomed to die soon.

These thoughts were pushed back into the recesses of my brain as I ventured down the hall of the hospital to see my child, whose abysmal future had been laid out before me by medical staff who regarded him as a disposable entity.

As I peered through the glass, a nurse gestured to an incubator that held my baby.

The day after

My heart immediately burst. He was beautiful with his pursed little mouth and furrowed little brow. I watched his chest rise and fall as he struggled for every breath, perhaps contemplating life or death.

I felt like I would faint from the sadness of it all. This wasn't a monster to be locked away on an island. Here was a sweet and helpless baby.

Between sobs, I saw that he looked a little bit like me, a little bit like his dad, and a little bit like our Chinese neighbors.

CHAPTER TWENTY-TWO

DELIVERING THE NEWS

We cried a river of tears

The next day, as my son awaited his mother's love, I flew to Las Vegas. Jean had worked her magic securing a last-minute seat on a direct flight that would land at 11 p.m.

I was going back with a broken heart, empty inside after giving birth. Like a thief in the night, I had crept away, leaving a defenseless baby while I went to stab his father in the heart.

It was a bumpy flight, and once again, I threw up the entire way. The cabin crew fawned over me after learning of my recent hospital stay.

Glenn was already at work when I arrived, so waiting for me when I landed at McCarran Airport was my stunning girlfriend Lorna, who happened to be a call girl. She and the drummer in the band shared our three-bedroom apartment. Strange as this seemed, it worked well. The four of us communed in harmony, and we each lived our separate lives.

The band was aware of my pending arrival, and they encouraged their unsuspecting leader to head straight home, conspiring to give us some privacy in our grief.

It was 1 a.m. when I heard the car door. Glenn walked in and stopped mid-stride, shocked to see me.

"Linda. . .what the hell?" he gasped as his eyes widened and flicked over me, uncomprehending.

"What. . .what are you doing here.? Oh my God, what is going on?"

He struggled to grasp the significance of my being there as I stood, immobile, unable to talk. Large tears formed and then slid down my face as he stared in alarm.

"What's the matter? Where is Christopher?"

Rushing toward me, he grabbed me by the shoulders.

"Is the baby here too?" Pleading with me, he said, "What's happening?"

I sobbed. "Glenn, I couldn't tell you on the phone. Our baby is very sick; he is dying." It was a surreal moment for both of us. The last time he saw me was less than three days ago when I was thirty pounds heavier with a baby bump. And now here I was, looking like I had never been pregnant, as my dancer's body had already bounced back.

I saw the shock on his face as he staggered back, uncomprehending. Words formed in his mouth, but he was unable to voice them.

Between sobs, I struggled to make sense of my own presence in Las Vegas when just the day before I was in a hospital bed in another country. I can only imagine the horror and confusion as the gravity of my words slowly took shape and sank in.

Stunned, he fell to the couch, his head in his hands. The state of our baby's health was spelled out in a rush of words. I described all that I had been told. Our newborn baby was in serious condition and not expected to live, and although he was profoundly disabled, he was a beautiful little boy who would melt your heart, though the doctors said it was best if we didn't bond with him.

We cried a river of tears together.

Neither Glenn nor I drank much, but at some point that night, as though in a trance, he went to the cupboard and poured a tumbler full of brown liquid and gulped it down. Then he poured another.

Before long the sobs subsided, and he fell into a deep sleep, while his postpartum wife, whose progesterone levels were in the tank collapsed beside him into nightmares of falling and never reaching the ground.

Early the next morning, casino management was notified that Glenn would not be finishing the contract that was due to end in three days. Our baby was in serious condition, and we needed to leave right away. Overnight, the band had hitched our trailer to the car and solemnly packed our belongings.

Word spread like wildfire as we made plans to leave, but our phone remained eerily silent. People were shocked and saddened. No doubt they didn't know what to say.

What do you say to a couple whose baby, born with multiple disabilities, was dying?

"It's for the best."

"He will soon be in God's hands."

"Go have another and forget about this one."

These words would be imparted all too often in the weeks ahead.

CHAPTER \ TWENTY-THREE

THE RETURN TO CANADA

*Hello, little guy, we're your parents. Yes, one of us
abandoned you, but we're here now.*

May 19 was a beautiful spring day in Las Vegas, but we
hardly noticed as we headed for Toronto, knowing we would
be facing a grueling 2,500 miles of heartache over the next
three days and nights.

By virtue of our child's diagnosis, we were now embarking on a road less traveled that was certain to be filled with
twists and turns and gut-wrenching decisions. We silently
considered what lay ahead, knowing that each divergent path
would take us on a different course of action.

It was now four days since our son was born, and I was
filled with intense guilt as I thought about how this precious
little soul was fighting for his life. A great aching weight filled

my heart as I considered my hasty decision to jump on a plane and run to his father's side.

It was quiet in the car as the wheels churned along the highway. There were hours when Glenn and I didn't say a word to each other, as we were both deep in our own thoughts and fears.

At times I pretended to be hopeful, as though eternal optimism would win the day, as it had for the past ten years of my frenetic life. And then reality would once more take over.

Surely the medical team at the hospital was talking about how I abandoned our helpless newborn son, who they must be referring to as Baby Boy Smith.

I couldn't share with anyone, especially Glenn, the excruciating pain in my heart. The guilt was overwhelming as I contemplated how I had run away after seeing this little soul struggling for breath. As the miles clicked by, I struggled to rationalize my decision.

I couldn't be blamed for wanting to tell his father the news in person.

Yes, I could. I chose to leave.

Why didn't I send Glenn's brother to give him the news and drive back with him? Had I even considered that? What if my son drew his last breath in the hospital with only strangers to send him on his way? Was Jean with him right now? Was he alone? Oh, please take this pain away.

There was plenty of time while we were driving for Glenn and I to discuss how this might have happened. Glenn mentioned that he had had premonitions of disaster during my pregnancy, and I wasn't shocked to hear him say this.

Glenn was an interesting blend of confidence and angst, who tended to view life as a cup half-empty. He was always waiting for the other shoe to drop, always looking over his shoulder wondering if the sky was going to fall.

I, on the other hand, was Pollyanna on steroids. My cup was always filled to the brim and spilling over. I was no withering flower. I had kicked into gear and jumped on a plane to Canada while in my eighth month of pregnancy, hadn't I? That was so typically me. So why was I second-guessing myself now?

Because I left a dying baby!

I thought about how in the lottery called life some people were winners and some weren't. I wondered why this had happened to us. The odds were one in eight hundred. Although we often cast our fate to the wind heading off to unknown places, we were also cautious in all our decisions. Neither of us were gamblers. We understood that we simply would not win on a game of chance.

We had planned for this baby. How could one little chromosome have randomly snuck in? The medical team said it was a fluke. So why us?

Thankfully, neither of us blamed the other. I had already heard that eighty-five percent of marriages fell apart when faced with the addition of a disabled child.

We talked till we were numb, at times resolving a point, then realizing we didn't know what would happen. We did not have a crystal ball. No one did.

A few hours into the trip, I glanced in the mirror on the visor and saw an unrecognizable face looking back at me. The pain in my heart was already aging me.

The mood on the drive was oppressive, fluctuating from grief to anger, to regret and shame. Occasionally I felt a moment of acceptance, but it was fleeting.

Would this baby forgive me for not staying by his side when he needed a mother's love the most? Oh, please, God, don't let him die. I want to hold him and tell him how sorry I am.

I also wondered if I would ever be able to forgive myself.

As we passed towns, RV parks, motels, orchards, farms, and cornfields, we each envisioned the meeting that would soon take place.

Hello, little guy, we're your parents. Yes, one of us abandoned you, but we're here now.

Occasionally we would stop along the way to change drivers and stretch our legs and aching backs in an ill-advised effort to drive straight though. We didn't notice the beauty of this country that we loved so much; instead we were caught up in trying to decipher each other's mood and asked what the other was thinking.

Sporadically we stopped for a quick meal or at the random roadside fruit stand. While at one particular stand, a sweet gentleman engaged us in conversation as we picked through his offerings.

"Where are you folks heading?"

To which for some unfathomable reason I sputtered, "To a hospital in Toronto to see our baby before he dies. . .I left him there."

My shocking announcement set Glenn back on his heels, and his face drained of all color. After I spoke those words, the man, who had crinkly eyes and a crumpled nose, leaned forward, and his gnarled brown hands shyly placed a pear firmly in my hands, accompanied by the kind and gentle words, "God will take care of everything. . .You will get there in time, there's no need to rush."

I appreciated his kindness, but through my tears a cynical, voice in my head said, *Really? Because God hasn't done such a great job of taking care of things so far.*

We thanked him for his generosity and climbed back in the car. As we got back on the road, we both broke down and cried. I had spoken the unspeakable, and our good long cry was a cathartic cleansing that left us feeling unburdened. What I had said now emboldened me.

We discussed all our options, realizing we were no longer walking the same path we had enjoyed for so many years. It was going to be different now, and there was no use looking back at what could have been.

Our conversation turned to the many practical matters that we now faced.

If our sick child lived, would I stay home with him while Glenn traveled?

How expensive would the medical care be that our son would need?

Should I move my mother and sister in with us to help with his care?

Should we get him christened right away?

Could we travel with a special-needs child?

What about his education? Were there special schools in Las Vegas for our boy?

What should we tell our friends? We knew of no other family with a disabled child. Would people understand?

What if he passed away? What would the funeral arrangements look like?

"It's my fault," I said. "I must have done something to cause this to happen. . . My crappy childhood must have had something to do with it. Maybe it was my strenuous dancing."

It's not your fault," said Glenn.

It was particularly kind of Glenn not to blame me, as it is a longstanding cultural tradition in North America to blame the mothers. As we reassured each other, we drew closer.

We were ignorant of the truth that having a child born with a disability is a genetic crapshoot. In the meantime, we traveled forward, misinformed, confused, and devastated, discussing a hundred scenarios.

We had so many questions. At every fork in the road, we had to choose a path. As we drove and drove and the miles clicked away, we continued to talk about the uncertain future.

We were unclear when we began this journey, but as we continued to head northeast toward the hospital, we developed a clear plan and purpose.

When we got to the hospital we would hold our baby tightly in our arms and love him until he passed peacefully away, or was well enough to come home with us.

We were going to tell him how sorry his mother was that she had left him behind. And we were going to tell him his name, the one we had chosen for a good and sweet boy. We were going to tell him that he was our Christopher.

CHAPTER TWENTY-FOUR

HELLO BABY CHRISTOPHER

He came into the world with opponents,
and I let them in.

Arriving in the Intensive Care Unit, I felt all eyes on Glenn and me. We must have been quite a sight: Glenn adorned with all the flashy accoutrements of an entertainer, gold neck chain, sideburns, long hair, and startling blue eyes, and me, a blonde in the requisite stiletto heels of a performer. We were not your typical new parents.

Calling Jean from the border, she gave us good news: although Christopher was still in intensive care, the medical team had upgraded his diagnosis and there was optimism about his chance for survival. He had been taken off life support and was now breathing on his own. He had also taken a bottle and was delighting the hospital staff. It appeared Christopher was a fighter. He was a miracle.

When we arrived, we announced ourselves at the nursery door, and we were quickly ushered over to our baby's bassinet.

I was ashamed when I saw his name "Baby Boy Smith" and birthdate affixed to his bed. He was so tiny, and we were in awe. Tears trickled down my face as he gazed at us with wise and astonishing blue eyes and pursed his little rosebud lips.

Who was this child who had caused me to rush thousands of miles away with bad news? Why had I been so devastated by this beautiful child? Why was his loveliness not apparent to me a few scant days before?

He came into the world with opponents, and I let them in. I should have defended him and not allowed them to impose such a bleak, depressing, fatal sentence on him.

Why had I allowed them to proclaim his quality of life so callously? What was so terrible that we must move to an island, segregated from the rest of society?

Every child was unique; this one had something extra. An additional chromosome. . .this one crazy random thing that determined his future and ours. Yes, we needed to hear about his medical issues, but for medical professionals to dictate the quality of our life as a family now appeared intrusive and cruel.

How did he know that this child would break up our marriage, or that society would reject us? Was that really up to a doctor to determine? What was I thinking in not giving him his chosen name, was it really because he wasn't worthy of it?

Glenn had not spoken a word as he appraised this little child. I found the silence unsettling as I waited to hear what he had to say about his offspring.

Several minutes went by before Glenn reached into the bassinet. Then, marveling as he picked him up, he said with a slight tremor in his voice, "This is my son, Christopher. He looks just like me. Let's get him out of here."

And we did.

A room for the baby in both our Rosedale home in Toronto and our Las Vegas apartment was always in the plans. My mother, my sister Jean, and Jean's son, Steven, shared our home in Canada. Now instead of leaving the baby's room empty, as we had recently been forced to contemplate, we were heading home with our Christopher, and a makeshift bassinette was hastily assembled.

The first order of business was to arrange a christening in the beautiful little church just down the street so we could give him his chosen name. For as long he was with us, he would be Christopher.

Our baby was by no means out of the woods. Before leaving the hospital, we met briefly with his pediatric cardiologist and discussed a litany of problems. He had many health issues and, of course, his cognitive state was yet to be determined. We were assured that "He will be a vegetable. If he manages to live past these first few years, he will never have a normal life. He most certainly won't live to ten years of age."

This news was relayed by a heart specialist with gloomy eyes and a perpetual frown, who said Christopher was born with two holes in his heart that would have to be monitored, with a possible surgery on the horizon. We were cautioned to pay close attention to his every breath, as he could suffer heart failure. In addition to this congenital heart defect, he had respiratory and intestinal problems.

In the meantime, he and we by extension, would live in the black and white of Oz where there existed no road to the magical, colorful Emerald City.

When I think back on those days, I want to go to the hospital and punch the face of every doctor who routinely predicted a quality of life for their child that sent parents scurrying down the "institutional route." That careless attitude is what led to the total segregation and abandonment of some of the most maligned and misunderstood people in history.

At the other extreme, friends tentatively called and told us stories about Down syndrome children, speaking reverentially that we had given birth to an angel, a messenger from God.

We were having none of it. Despite the cardiovascular issues and the intellectual disability, our baby like all newborns was beautiful. But he was also a little destroyer of dreams and hopes, of plans that had now gone awry.

Our initial feelings were of shock, disbelief and terror—the future we expected for our son had disappeared in a second, and we grieved for the child that might have been. We didn't want to hear the placating opinions of friends. We were the ones who were stuck with the problem. No one was offering to take him off our hands. It was confusing. Friends and family, although concerned about our situation, seemed drawn in by our little guy. But when we took him out to the store or park, people would stare, or worse, avert their eyes and turn away.

Life was unpredictable, and we took one day at a time. Chris needed to be closely monitored. He could live a few days, a month, a year, maybe more. The medical professionals said there was no way to know if he could thrive with all his issues. One member of the medical team said "It would be best if the child dies sooner." Chris grew on us each day, and all we could think was that even a few years would be better than just the few hours the doctor predicted the day he was born.

One day, a friend gave me a beautiful essay by Emily Perl Kingsley, called "Welcome to Holland" that was based on her own experience of having a child with Down syndrome. The essay was thought-provoking and meant to paint a picture for new parents that there was grace and beauty involved in the journey with a disabled child.

The essay was a metaphor for the "change of plans" when a child was unexpectedly born disabled. She likened it to planning a trip to Italy and landing instead in Holland, only to find that Holland wasn't a bad place. It wasn't Italy, but it had its own beauty.

As much as I wanted to embrace this idea that my kiddo took me on a journey to Holland and introduced me to Rembrandts, tulips, and windmills, what I really wanted was to be in Italy, hang out with all the beautiful people and see the Colosseum, the Vatican, and the Amalfi Coast. Deep down, I was angry.

How was I supposed to navigate through Holland? What did I need to do to get to Italy? Was this fate? Why, why, why did this happen to me? What will this poor child have to endure in life? Should we wait to see if he lives before we consider having another one? If a brother or sister enters the picture, would they be teased, or would they resent their sibling because they must help with the care?

All the research that was available in the medical journals on my trips to the library showed the most grotesque conditions—a tomb with no way out.

But here was Christopher, at home in a loving and nurturing environment, and he set about defying the doctors' orders. He prevailed and chugged on, his extra chromosome carrying the day. *Up syndrome,* I thought. My positive outlook returned; my optimism would sustain him.

But I still had to forgive myself for wanting him to die.

CHAPTER TWENTY-FIVE

FOREVER MY SON'S CHAMPION

Will you ruin my life forever more?
Is there a reason you were born to me?

If I had known that I was carrying a disabled child, a defective baby who would need a lifetime of care, would I have terminated the pregnancy. I shuddered to think of that option.

I didn't want this child. When he was born, I turned away from him, and literally took flight. I asked God to take him from me. Return him from whence he came. I willed him away. I had a legitimate excuse to run from him, and I hoped he would be gone when I returned.

How does one ever reconcile those thoughts?

As I stared in wonder at this child who regarded me with an intensity that took my breath away, I wondered if he could look into my heart and see these secrets known only to me.

His beautiful blue eyes fixed on me and held an intelligence that captivated me.

Were they certain he had Down syndrome?

But he did. He had the characteristics - a thicker neck fold, simian creases on both palms, and slanted eyes that belied his otherwise perfect appearance. Eventually a blood test confirmed the doctor's early prognosis.

A "genetic crapshoot," they said. Would anyone have a child if they were given the statistics of how many children are born with disabilities?

I was incredibly sorry for my abandonment, but forgiveness would be a long time coming.

Friends and family came to the house and took turns holding our little snuggle bun, some with faces of abject pity, others with kindness and hopefulness, accepting the randomness of life and extolling his virtues. My boy made our friends and family both laugh and cry, and they accepted him into their hearts. Slowly, I accepted him into mine, at times regarding him from a distance.

Is there a reason you were born to me? Will you ruin my life forever?

We had been so blind to life's arbitrary ways. One day the world was revolving slowly and purposely; the next minute it came crashing down like a meteor, destroying everything in its path.

But something strange and unexpected started to happen. As I peered deeply into Chris' eyes, I began to feel a connection.

Our baby was accepted by our show biz friends, like the legendary comedian and actress Gilda Radner, who made funny faces at our boy and laughed wildly at his expressions.

He had loose joints and no muscle tone, so his little body would just flop over. He couldn't hold his bottle, so he waited patiently; gazing up with complete trust that someone would feed him.

We knew that we'd be his caregivers for as long as he lived. Even if he lived beyond the doctor's predictions, he would never go to college, father children, find adventures in far places. He wouldn't be successful in the way society thinks it matters. He wouldn't run for office, play football, follow in his parents' footsteps, or buy his old mom and dad a house one day.

Having a child with a profound disability was a lifetime commitment of care. He would stay close by our side, and we would fight for his rights for as long as he was with us. After he reached a certain intellectual age, he would remain there as if frozen in time. I wondered if he would ever be able to speak clearly or ever call me Mom.

At first, each day with Christopher was a nightmare. There was so much misinformation out there, and I was constantly fact-checking and looking for other parents to talk to who could allay my fears brought on by ignorance.

On my darkest days when reality came crashing down, it felt like someone was repeatedly bashing my head in with a club. There were nights those first six months when I wailed and implored God to make sense of this child's birth. I would beat my chest and howl at the moon. Seeing my perpetual state of anguish, well-meaning people suggested I give Chris to the state.

"It is the right thing to do. Keeping him with you will ruin your life. You will not be able to do all the things that you planned to do. He will always need babysitters even as an adult. He will need constant, twenty-four-hour care. It's understandable that you would look at options. No one would blame you."

Sympathetic gestures abounded as we reconnected with our peers and far-flung friends. I tried to explain that this little fellow was coaching me in kindness. That he had opened my heart and given me a sensitivity that until then had not revealed itself. People nodded encouragingly, and though they didn't say anything, I could see their relief as they thought, "Thank God this is not my life."

Some people insinuated that we caused our son's disability. That was of course just plain ignorance, but it was prevalent, and it stank. Sometimes strangers, even acquaintances, would meet Chris and imitate his grimaces and flap their hands. It was fascinating to watch how they inadvertently dealt with their own discomfort.

Was I guilty of this, too?

I remember a family in England, who lived a few streets away from us, who had a strange-looking child who would sometimes be in the front garden. I was so frightened of this poor soul that I avoided passing by the house whenever the child was outside.

Chris taught me tolerance. I learned not to react so instinctively to people's insensitivity, and instead feel sorry for their ignorance. But that didn't stop me from being terrified by the enormous emotional and financial responsibility of having to care for him. Studies predicted that a child with intellectual and related disabilities costs a family over $2 million in lifetime care.

Early on, a social worker who heard about Chris' birth made an appointment to stop by our house. She said handing a child over to the government would not absolve me of perpetual self-loathing, guilt, doubt, and a lifetime of heartache.

We inquired about receiving a little bit of help, and we quickly found out that it's all or nothing. You either turned your child over to the government for lifelong care, or you took him home and bore all the costs. That was stupid, because it was exponentially more expensive to institutionalize a child than to help parents out.

We read an article by ethicist Joseph Fletcher who, two years before Christopher was born, wrote in the *Atlantic Monthly* that "There was no reason to feel guilty about putting a Down syndrome baby away, whether in a sanatorium or in a more responsible lethal sense. Yes it was dreadfully sad, but it carried no guilt. True guilt arose only when an offense was committed against another person, and a Down's child was not a person."

I was outraged when I heard those opinions spoken and written by people who never experienced having a child with a disability, who would never know the fierce and protective love of a parent.

I was often mad at God.

How much could be heaped on one person? Didn't I deserve a good life after surviving the abuse at the hands of my father?

On a very dark day, Glenn and I took a trip to see some of the state-sanctioned facilities for children on the list we'd been given. What we saw was horrific and gut-wrenching. Hundreds of abandoned children with mental and physical disabilities were locked up like human litter, isolated from families and society at large, living with paid staff.

We observed some children with extreme medical issues who needed intensive care, but most of the kids were like our son. We visited one overcrowded facility where the children were all under the age of ten and without exception, in cribs. Some stood holding their arms out, imploring us to rescue them; others stared glassy-eyed at a point above our heads. If they were labeled intellectually disabled at birth, they could now add environmentally disabled and abandoned to the list.

Their disabilities sentenced these children to a life on death row. But for them there was no appeal or constitutional rights of protection, no one to advocate for them. Here the most vulnerable and neglected children were subjected to the worst abuse.

Visiting these institutional settings was the most distressing thing I had ever witnessed or hoped to witness. We wanted to grab each one of these poor souls and run and never look back. We came home that day and hugged our little guy and vowed that we would never desert him. He would grow up with family, knowing that he was loved. I would never get the image of those children out of my mind. That visit had a major impact on my future life.

I was a slow learner, but in time, I came to believe that Chris was born to me due to some cosmic force evoked by God. That would explain his pure heart and where he had learned to love with such abandon. He brought to earth an interstellar knowledge beyond human understanding. His life had more meaning than I could possibly comprehend at that point.

I now belonged to a special club of five hundred million people, fifteen percent of the population worldwide, who had given birth to a child that was considered a catastrophe, not just by the medical team, but by his own family. The professionals had laid out a depressing future that understandably caused much pain and anger at God and at him for being born.

But soon, Christopher defied the doctors' predictions, and he was no longer in permanent proximity to death. My anger eventually dissipated and it was replaced by an all-consuming love. He was our responsibility, he needed our help, and yet, like the Anne Murray song "You Needed Me," we soon found out we needed him a whole lot more.

I must admit that I often felt pangs of jealousy as friends touted the remarkable accomplishments of their children riding a bike, reading at an advanced level, being toilet trained and walking at age one.

Those things were remarkable to me, because something that might have sounded so simple pre-Christopher was now seemingly genius in other children.

Forever my son's champion

I was consumed by fear for his future.

How could he live without the help of a constant caregiver? Who would that person be when his father and I were no longer around to care for him? Who would care that his glass of water had to be exactly three inches from the right of the nightstand?

On a cool October day when Christopher was six months old, the light came on. . . and it stayed on. Bundled up in his blue parka, his little face and crystal blue eyes sparkled, and his mysterious smile beckoned me to love him, as his pure, innocent love enveloped me.

It was then that I had the revelation that he was mine. He didn't just happen to me; he was given to me. I was to be his protector, his champion, his guardian, and his advocate. Most of all, I was to be the mother of a most unique and special child. Yes, he had Down syndrome and a plethora of conditions that came with it, but I would make sure the diagnosis did not define my child.

Christopher was special and his life had meaning. He would not be condemned by a medical team to institutional life or be put aside due to society's misguided norms. He was my quirky little boy. He would live an amazing life. He could be who he wanted to be—my son.

CHAPTER TWENTY-SIX

LET'S RENT A BARN AND PUT ON A PARTY

It was my very first fundraising event, and it was a sellout.
My son was changing my life.

Shortly after Christopher's birth, it became abundantly clear that there was very little in the way of information and support for parents of a disabled child. Christopher was born in the era following the mass deinstitutionalization of so many poor souls whose fate had been determined by either society's revulsion or by medical professionals, whether they were well-meaning or not,

Folks with intellectual disabilities had been neglected, misunderstood, undervalued, and abused since the beginning of time. As recently as the 1960s, people deemed feeble-minded were subject to unethical human experimentation in the United States and in other countries.

For decades, mentally disabled children at the Willowbrook State School in New York had been deliberately infected with hepatitis in the medical community's search for a vaccine. Participation in the study was a condition for admission to the institution.

The Salk vaccine was injected into institutionalized children and adults to test its effects as a cure for polio. Radioactive oatmeal was served up to determine the results of constant exposure to radiation. Other experiments included the exposure of mentally disabled individuals to chemical and biological weapons, including deadly or debilitating diseases.

Funding for many of the experiments was provided by the United States government, the United States military, and the CIA. The ethical, professional, and legal implications of this in the medical and scientific community were quite significant and led to public outrage in the late twentieth century.

None of those depressing, inhumane institutions would exist if more support and information were given to beleaguered families. Much misinformation was given at birth, and many parents made choices out of fear and ignorance. We could attest to that after we were told we should move to an island.

I felt bad for parents who felt compelled to abandon their disabled children. It wasn't their fault; it's what the medical community and society encouraged.

When Christopher was born, we were told, "If you take him home, you will be alienated from your friends and society. And what will happen to him if he outlives you?" It was a horrifying prospect to contemplate.

But that is exactly what has come to pass. For the first time in history, children like our son were outliving their families and caregivers.

If that happened to us, who would know or care that Christopher liked his oats mashed with honey yogurt, that he didn't like showers, that he loved bubbles in his bath, and that the water must be tepid?

For too long, people with complex disabilities were judged as subhuman. They were ostracized, shut away, and hidden. We were told that our son was disposable, human detritus, like the trash we throw away each day.

Discovering the lack of support made us hold Christopher tighter. It was a slow process, but we were coming to terms with the birth of our boy. We were no longer shattered; we adored our little wrecker.

As I continued on this journey as my son's mom, I began to realize I could not imagine a world without people like my boy in it. We would champion his unique ability to give a boundless and limitless amount of love without asking for anything in return. We would tell all who would listen how much potential he and others like him had. We would give him a chance to live his life, and fight for his rights as a citizen of the world. I would encourage others to think differently about the disabled.

Still in Canada and needing to work, I had to find help with Christopher. I looked at daycare facilities, and was shocked to learn that not one would accept my son due to his disability.

Again I was struck by the fact that people didn't understand the issues related to having a diagnosis of mental retardation. Chris had defied the doctors' orders and lived. Why now was he excluded from daycare? He wasn't sick, he wasn't ill, he wasn't contagious. He simply had a medical condition called Down syndrome.

It soon became clear that there was no help available, at least not the kind I was looking for.

I envisioned starting a daycare program where "mainstream kids" were allowed, even encouraged, to play and interact with special-needs kids. There must be acceptance and tolerance on both sides. By doing this, mainstream children would learn valuable lessons about the unique and special qualities of children like my Chris.

I knew that in order to make my daycare dream come true, I needed to raise funds. But other than performing at a myriad of charitable benefits events during my career, I had no idea how to raise money for a worthy cause. I would have to figure that out on my own.

I decided that my first foray into the world of philanthropy would be to produce and direct a concert, enlisting the help of the many show-biz people in my Rolodex.

And so I embarked on the next phase of my life, the most meaningful and most rewarding phase as an activist mom.

This mission to secure a place for the concert and pay nothing for it became an obsession of mine. Charities solve society's problems, and everyone needed to be charitable, including the venue operators. This conviction about the importance of a charity keeping all fundraising dollars earned served me well in my new career, a career that had never crossed my mind prior to Chris' birth.

I was a performer, not a show producer. I also knew nothing about the nonprofit sector. What I did know was that there were many problems in the world, and if society turned a blind eye, people in need would be left out in the cold.

As phone calls were made, I found that telling a sad story was not the way to get people to join your cause. Instead they would hug their children closer and give thanks that they had escaped the genetic crapshoot.

People were much more interested in jumping on a train that was going somewhere interesting and exciting. On each call I spelled out my vision, what the finish line would look like, and how their support would make all the difference. I presented a simple concept that people could get behind.

Enlisting our friend Gilda Radner, who was currently appearing in the Toronto production of *Godspell*, was a stroke of genius because she then enlisted her *Godspell* co-stars, Martin Short and Paul Shaffer.

Musicians like Ronnie Hawkins, who was highly influential in the establishment of rock music in Canada; Levon Helm, the drummer for The Band; and the cast of the Canadian musical TV series, *Pig and Whistle*, along with many local celebrities, also jumped on the bandwagon.

Everything fell into place when the Oshawa Civic Center agreed to donate the venue, along with the lights and sound.

My son was changing my life.

CHAPTER TWENTY-SEVEN

THE BORDER

This boy loved going places.

Christopher's entry into our lives, which had at first been rejected, was now rejoiced. He was our magical boy, his extra chromosome bringing extra love. Our lives were turned upside down when he was born; now we felt we had won the lottery.

At eighteen months, Christopher loved going places. He happily blew kisses and gurgled joyfully, as he was tucked into his baby seat, wearing a fluffy, pastel-blue jumper that complimented his upward slanting, bluest-of-blue eyes.

We were up early on December 22, 1972, excited to drive from Toronto to a holiday concert appearance in Syracuse, New York, then on to Las Vegas. It was frustrating having to wait precious hours for the snow and sleet to stop. A travel advisory reported dangerous road conditions and warned us to stay put, but staying put was not an option.

Our working life as traveling entertainers meant that we were continuously on the road, crisscrossing North and South America, Europe and Asia with Glenn and the band performing in venues as far away as Thailand and the U.K.

The next job was nearly 300 miles southeast of the U.S. border in Syracuse, New York, and we needed to get going in order to arrive in time for a very lucrative, limited engagement. We simply didn't have the luxury of staying nice and cozy in front of the fire in the loving home of Glenn's parents that was filled with holiday cheer.

As we pulled out of the driveway into the snowstorm, anxious family members cautioned us to drive safe as we headed toward the U.S./Canadian border at Niagara Falls.

Our recently purchased Oldsmobile Toronado pulled a small utility trailer full of amplifiers, guitars, banjos, drums and a sound system. The car's blue and silver Nevada license plates sported the moniker SMITH, and we loved that Steve McQueen's 1966 film, *Nevada Smith*, connected us to the state we called home.

It was the 1970s, the time of the "Great Inflation." The stock market was a mess, interest rates had skyrocketed to twenty percent, unemployment was high, and hundreds of our soldiers were dying in the steamy jungles of Vietnam each week, while many of the young boys who returned were mentally and/or physically broken and disillusioned.

Very few people on the road had Nevada license plates, especially attached to a shiny bronze car and matching trailer with the words "Vegas or Bust: emblazoned on the back bumper which made us quite the spectacle. We didn't mind. We were proud to be card-carrying Americans and in particular Las Vegans, and we flaunted it.

Christmas was just days away, and our car was laden with surprises that had been lovingly bought and tucked away in various places unwrapped lest border officials suspected they were illegal.

The border

Among the gifts was a musical toy for Christopher and Bushnell binoculars for his dad. Glenn had planned our trip west after Syracuse to include a night at the Grand Canyon on our way to Las Vegas, and he would be delighted to receive the field glasses.

Wrapping paper and bows were also stuffed into the vehicle's crevasses, along with a tiny, folding, plastic Christmas tree, which would be discarded after the holiday.

Goodies lovingly baked by Glenn's mom were arranged on platters. There was one tray for us to enjoy during the drive, another for when we arrived at our hotel, and a larger platter to share with the band. These delectable creations were giving off an irresistible aroma, begging to be consumed that very moment.

In a short time, we found ourselves in the middle of a quagmire as busses, trucks, and cars faced off against the storm of the century. Our hitched trailer made the perilous storm even more dangerous.

People showed up to help push the vehicles that were stuck in the snow off the road. We estimated that what should have been a 90-minute drive to the border would take at least four-hours.

As we got closer to the entrance to the Lewiston Border Crossing, Christopher, who had been sleeping in the back seat, woke up, and we entertained him by singing Elton John's newly released hit song, "Rocket Man":

We sang with fervent unrestrained enthusiasm because the louder our voices were, the more joyous the noises that came out of Christopher's little bow-shaped lips as he tried to sing along *oooohahhhhhoooo. . . okkokkimahhhhh*.

We got in the shortest line, hoping the guard would be the least likely to detain us with unnecessary questions. With our international green card permits denoting our status in the U.S. in our hands, we contemplated the likelihood of better weather and smoother sailing once we crossed the border.

UNWANTED

Interstate 90 on the American side was a well-travelled, direct route to our destination, and we would pick up some of the time already lost on this trip.

The last time I crossed the border at this check point, little notice had been taken of our little bundle. But this time when our car came to a full stop at the United States border at Niagara Falls, the border official took one look at Christopher and decided his fate.

CHAPTER TWENTY-EIGHT

UNDESIRABLE

*What was it about our sweet little boy that had
this guy on high alert?*

We stood inside the ugly, drafty, two-room building at the U.S. border that was no more than a freezing shack. Snow flurries whirled outside, while the north wind relentlessly rattled the door. We were sequestered inside an immigration office on the Lewiston Bridge at Niagara Falls on the U.S. side of the border in the State of New York, and I was steaming mad.

As entertainers, we had been subjected to many searches over the years during our world travels, including going from Toronto to Las Vegas. Entertainers were routinely viewed as likely smugglers of contraband.

Two years prior, when I was pregnant with Christopher, we crossed the border into Detroit with an entourage of bandmates. It was a beautiful sunny day that quickly turned into a five-hour confrontation resulting in the car's back seat being removed and the carpet being taken out of the trunk of our car.

That time at least five border officials strip-searched our car and the cars belonging to our band members, certain they would find drugs or other smuggled goods.

They ended up confiscating three tuxedos that were several years old that had been tailor-made in Las Vegas, alleging we had not paid taxes on the suits when we brought them into Canada, and they wanted us to pay a fine for importing goods without paying duty. If we didn't pay a fine, we wouldn't get the suits back. We couldn't afford the fine and the suits were not worth the cost of the duty, so we told the guards to keep them, afraid they might plant an illegal substance on us to justify their action. In the ensuing years, we had many a laugh as we pictured our antagonists wearing the lost tuxedos adorned with beads and sequined lapels.

But now here we were in a much more serious situation. This wasn't about hippie, druggie entertainers or a car filled with contraband.

The red-faced border officer was clearly repulsed as he stood glaring at our eighteen-month-old son, while Christopher, who had been extricated from his warm and comfy car seat and brought into this grim, unfriendly place, cooed in his goofy way.

Secure in his position as an official of the United States government, the guard announced that he brought us into the office so he could explain the laws regarding the transportation of undocumented aliens. He was talking about our 18-month-old son.

Christopher, who was bundled up in his blue onesie parka, smiled at the guy, sweetly blowing bubbles and kisses his way. Glenn and I grew more frustrated and angry by the minute as he regarded our baby with distain.

Transporting? What the hell! The word implied the smuggling of illegal goods from one place to another. We had never come across such open loathing.

What was it about our sweet little boy that had this guy on high alert?

Since Chris' birth eighteen months earlier, we had traveled back and forth across the border without any concern, simply showing our immigration identification cards to bored officials. Chris was usually sleeping in his bassinet when we crossed to the other side and drew no attention. Now we were face to face with someone who was set on sending our baby back from where he came.

Our instinct as our son's protectors was to punch the man in the face and leave. We, however, would be in deep trouble if we struck a man in uniform carrying a badge and a gun, which were both on full display on his ample belly. This man had the full weight of the United States Immigration Department behind him, and the power to ruin our lives.

Millions of people crossed borders around the world every day. Like most others, we did not take the security lightly. It was a daunting job, and we had a great deal of respect for the federal officers, who monitored the traffic looking for contraband and other illegal trafficking.

But it was becoming abundantly clear to us that we were being accused of committing a crime. A very serious situation was unfolding that we were powerless to stop.

The guard told us to sit in the corner while he called for backup. He moved into the other room and pulled out some paperwork, while standing in front of the only space heater in the place.

We didn't sit, as the space we presently occupied was exceedingly cold, and we needed to keep moving to stay warm. I watched Glenn's fists clench and unclench, and could see in his eyes that there would soon be a confrontation of dire consequences.

We had to stay calm and not play into this guy's game. He was hoping for a border incident where he could be the hero and save the country from a couple of Las Vegas ne'er-do-wells and their extra chromosome, blowing kisses infant.

If it hadn't been so unfair, it would have been funny.

"We will figure this out. Don't provoke the guy. He can revoke our green cards," I whispered to Glenn.

Eventually he came back to the outer office, and with eyes that never left our son, he announced, "You two are legal residents of the United States and are both holding Green Cards, but why don't you have one for him?"

Both Glenn and I were legal residents of the United States and had been for many years. We were tax-paying, flag-waving, Las Vegas homeowners. We were in possession of the most coveted A-1 Visa, sponsored by political and celebrity friends.

This designation was reserved for diplomats and other foreign government officials, including Heads of State, cabinet ministers, rocket scientists, and uniquely talented people. We were proud to be in such heady company.

We had also begun the process of U.S. citizenship, and, with Chris' birth, we were working on getting his immigration status approved. The paperwork had been sent in, and it was just a matter of time before we received it.

Understanding that he was attempting to provoke us, and knowing full well we didn't have a Green Card for Christopher, we carefully explained the circumstances of our immigration journey to date, facts that would enlighten him and cause him to let us continue our trip.

Glenn was Canadian-born, and I was British-born. We were both legal residents of the U.S. We possessed Green Cards, giving us legal immigration status in the U.S. where we lived. We had a home in Las Vegas and planned for Chris to be born there until a recent lucrative booking of an appearance at the Royal York Hotel was offered. The snafu occurred when Chris decided to start the birthing process a month early, during a short hop across the border, resulting in him being born at North York General, which made him a Canadian citizen.

We told this story hoping to influence the officer, but to no avail. He was not impressed, so we got back to business. Here was his birth certificate along with our American IDs. We had engaged an immigration attorney shortly after Christopher's birth and were now waiting for him to give us news of a special dispensation for our son. It should arrive at any time.

Our indifferent guard, accompanied now by an equally indifferent backup officer, coolly observed us, waiting for us to run out of words. It was icy cold in the office, and we continued stamping our feet while blowing air onto our frozen hands. The wind howled at the door, whispering. . .*YOU PEOPLE ARE SCREWED.*

While the snow softly fell, it became very clear that this guy was not going to let us go any time soon. As a matter of fact, he called for even more backup to attend to his duties outside while he dealt with us. We were going nowhere fast. We found out early on that our son had an acute sense for danger, and now his inquisitive blue eyes were imploring us to get out of this place.

"Let's get this show on the road, Mom."

As our antagonist emerged once more from his heated room, we took another tack, hoping to draw him into being the hero of the moment. We discussed the need to get moving: we had an arduous drive ahead of us, and it would be slow going with the snow piling up at the Buffalo/Niagara Border. We needed to leave now so we could get to our hotel before the roads became impassable. We threw in some of our most compelling arguments, reminding him that it was just two days before Christmas.

"Have you ever been to Las Vegas? It's a great city to visit. The hotels there have all-you-can-eat buffets that only cost three dollars. And we can often get much sought after showroom tickets."

His eyes flicked.

Damn. We were getting dangerously close to bribing this bozo. But by appealing to a more humane side of this man, we hoped he'd make the easy decision to keep this nice family together during the holidays.

But none of this mattered. Our son wasn't being discriminated against because of his lack of a Green Card. Christopher was being discriminated against because of his disability. He was being denied entry into the United States because he had Down syndrome.

We knew what was really on this man's mind. We had researched the laws after Chris' birth and understood that there were exclusionary circumstances for "certain classes of people." Unfortunately, our little guy was one of the "excluded."

A review of early immigration statutes revealed that, as far back as 1859, both Canadian and United States immigration laws consistently targeted classes of people, who, based on their perceived mental health, were automatically denied entry.

For over half a century, Canadian immigration legislation explicitly emphasized that "lunatics," "the insane," "the feeble-minded," and others of a similar ilk were not welcome into the U.S. or Canada. These outdated laws put our son in a unique category. He would need special dispensation.

If truth be told, at a recent meeting with our attorney, he suggested it could take time to get Christopher's visa approved due to his exclusionary disability status. We naively dismissed his concerns and merrily went on our way, crossing the border monthly since his birth. Chris was just a baby, and he was born to American residents. Glenn was a valued entertainer in the U.S., and we had many friends in the entertainment business including casino moguls, celebrities, even politicians who had written letters in support of a visa for him. Until that was granted, he would by law travel on our visas and passports until age eighteen.

We knew we were wasting our breath in that small, cold border office. Our pleas for compassion fell on deaf ears.

After rummaging around in his office, searching through large binders and documents, the guard returned and slammed a large binder on the counter.

"Section 212(a) of the immigration and naturalization act states that people exempt from entering the United States as permanent residents are, number one, criminals; number two, retarded people."

He rattled off some more excluded classes before taking a breath and pointing his finger at both of us.

"You are legally allowed into the country, but you need to get him out now," he said.

That was the end of the discussion. We were at his mercy, and he knew it.

Glenn drew back his arm and would have smashed the guy's face had I not restrained him. I had faced off against my son's detractors since his birth. Heaven knows I had been primed for it. Evil lurks in every corner, and I had hard-scrabbled my way through life and risen above every obstacle up to this moment. I would not lie down and give up just because a whole damn country rejected my child.

My son, the boy with no name whose bracelet proclaimed him simply "Baby Boy Smith," was now Christopher, and by God he was not going to be branded by ignorance, not if I had any say in the matter.

I quietly reasoned with Glenn that we should leave now and re-enter Canada. The longer we stayed in that office, the more likely he would find a reason to deny us entry as well.

We would get to a phone and call family to drive up from Toronto and get Chris. We would wait in a coffee shop in Niagara Falls on the Canadian side, and after we handed Chris over into the loving arms of family, we would proceed on to our job in Syracuse, and they could bring Chris over the following day. It was just one more day. There was not much that we could do here with this man.

We decided to call Christopher's nanny, Edith, to see if she and her husband, Art, would be interested in a trip to the border to retrieve him. They could spend the night in a hotel in Niagara Falls, or maybe take him to their home outside Toronto and return the next day, crossing the border on December 23rd. We would caution them to cross at Rainbow Falls, an alternative bridge. It was a longer route, but we assumed they wouldn't have to deal with our recent enemy, and it would be smooth sailing.

Edith and Art enjoyed traveling to our shows, and with this plan they could also have a little vacation and spend the evening in Syracuse enjoying dinner and a show before returning home for Christmas.

I steered Glenn, who was holding a smiling Christopher, back to the car. The guard lifted the rail, and we were forced to make a U-turn and go back the way we came.

Safely in the car with our Green Cards tucked away, I announced to the guard that we would be calling our attorney about this incident. He sneered at us and told us to get moving.

Like thieves in the night, we re-entered Canada with our little undesirable bundle, who took this all in with a wisdom known only to his Maker.

CHAPTER TWENTY-NINE

UNWANTED

At age eighteen months, my kiddo had a rap sheet.

After several hours and an emotional sendoff, we waved good-bye to our little guy and headed back to Syracuse and "The Den of the Little Foxes," knowing that Christopher would be back with us the following day.

Edith and Art had been willingly enlisted to spend the night in Niagara Falls, and early the next morning they would cross the border into the U.S.

Outraged and frustrated about what had just transpired, we headed back toward the border, once again driving through the blizzard, only this time we were fraught with anguish and heartache. Once again we had left our son behind.

After much discussion, we concluded that this border agent was just having a really bad day. Surely, this kind of treatment was an anomaly. We knew that we needed a special visa for Chris, but he was, after all, just a baby. In time the matter would resolve itself.

As we prepared for the Christmas Eve performance on the top floor of the Syracuse Hotel, we decorated our hotel room, placing our little pop-up Christmas tree on the coffee table alongside gifts and toys for Christopher, his baby bed, and a family photo. As always, we were going to have as normal a celebration as possible under the circumstances.

By now we had traveled full time for several years, and I had become quite adept at turning a 200-square-foot hotel room into a home. I could have given lessons on economizing suitcase space.

Once unpacked and organized, we settled in expecting that this limited engagement would be like every other. Glenn would knock 'em dead, thus ensuring a return invitation.

After a week's stay that would run through New Year's Eve, we would leave Syracuse and head to our next job in Cleveland, then Tulsa, Houston, Dallas, and finally on to Las Vegas and our newly purchased first home.

We awoke the next morning to a ringing phone. It was Art and Edith, our wonderful saviors who had agreed to bring Chris to us. In disbelief, we listened as a sobbing Edith said, "we are on our way back to our house with Chris. They were waiting for us at the Rainbow Falls border, and they wouldn't let us cross. They turned us back."

Bit by bit the story unfolded. As they pulled up to the crossing, a guard asked for their identification and then they asked for Christopher's. It quickly became clear that the guard was more interested in one little baby than he should have been. He took their credentials into the office where they could see a conversation taking place with several other guards.

When the guard came out, his hand was on his gun. He motioned for Edith and Al to move the car into the right lane and come into the office for further inspection. In less than twenty-four hours, Chris had been singled out twice.

Art and Edith complied. They bundled the baby up in their arms, and dutifully followed the guard into the border control office, where they were told to sit on chairs lined up against the wall.

Eventually, an officer beckoned them to follow him into another office.

Were they being arrested?

The men in uniform meant business. The Greens began to shake. They were respectable seniors, pillars of their community, and here they were in no man's land, held in an immigration office on the border of their country.

Surely this couldn't be about one baby needing to be with family for Christmas?

But it was. The officers read the charges.

It turned out our baby boy was on record with the United States Immigration and Naturalization Department as being an "undesirable alien." He was excluded from entry and branded so forever more. Art and Edith were being accused of aiding and abetting, attempting to smuggle a baby, who had already been rejected by the U.S.

The charges read out loud cited immigration violations that were punishable by fines and jail time. There would be a record of my undesirable alien at every point of entry, including ferry crossings, along the 3,855 square miles of borders and 219 border check points. At age eighteen months, my kiddo had a rap sheet and couldn't venture out of the country in which he was born.

In the end, The Green's were scolded for attempting another crossing with Christopher, and warned not try it again. Then they were sent back across the slippery wet bridge, back to Canada from whence they came, and another long trip home.

And here they were on the phone, in shock, sorrowfully explaining that they risked arrest if they attempted to cross again.

It was too much. We were in total disbelief.

Wallowing in self-pity would do nothing to solve the problem; something had to be done, but what? We would not sit back and allow the law to dictate whether or not we could live with our child. We had done nothing wrong. It was outrageous. We sat for a long time wrestling with indecision.

Glenn wanted to drive to the border and confront those guards. But what good would that do? He'd be arrested, and then we would really be screwed.

I suggested flying Chris in. Maybe the immigration officials at the airport wouldn't notice. Who could we get to do that? Or would we be putting another family member or friend in jeopardy?

Glenn was so angry he said we should leave and go back to Toronto to be with Chris. But that would be the last time this hotel would book us. And what about the band? They needed the job as much as we did.

We were divided in our opinion, frustrated by indecision. We needed the job and the money that came with it. But could we spend Christmas without our child?

Out of the confusion and anger, came indignation and the zeal to right the wrong. We had a responsibility not only to our child, but also to the nightclub owners and our band. Too many people would be affected by the wrong decision.

As Glenn explained the situation to the guys through gritted teeth, I began a frantic search for help. After calling our attorney in Canada and every other potential supporter we could think of, we had exhausted our connections. There had to be someone who could help.

I started leafing through the dog-eared yellow pages. I had no idea what I might find, but I forged on looking up the words "disabilities," "handicapped services," "Down syndrome," "mental retardation,"

Wait. . . Here was something: The Syracuse Association for Retarded Citizens, also known as Arc.

It was 3 p.m. on December 24th when I placed the call. I fully expected a recording. Instead a friendly voice answered.

"Syracuse Arc, can I help you?"

I briefly explained the situation to the woman on the other end of the line. While I was put on hold, I flashed back to the events of the last two days. Was it possible that children with disabilities were prevented from traveling across borders with their family? What if the family wanted to go to Disneyland? Would the disabled child be left behind?

A new voice came on the line. "This is Susan Morse, public relations director for the Arc of Syracuse New York. How may I be of service?"

Hearing a concerned, friendly voice, I dissolved into tears.

After relaying the entire story to a sympathetic Susan Morse, she had to go. It was nearing 5 p.m. on Christmas Eve, and she and the receptionist were the only people left in the building. She said she would do what she could, but at this late hour she wasn't certain that much could be accomplished. Before she hung up, she promised to get back to me.

That was it. . . there was nowhere else to turn. We felt dejected and overwhelmed. I had climbed many mountains in my life, but this one had the full force of the U.S. government at its front lines. It was a daunting wall.

It was 6:30 p.m. and we were listlessly prepared for a very important stage performance when we heard an unexpected knock on our hotel room door.

Upon opening it, we rocked back on our heels when a slew of news reporters and cameramen from NBC, CBS, ABC, *The Syracuse Post Standard* newspaper and other local news outlets pushed their way into our room. They crowded into the small space with cameras rolling, and microphones shoved in our faces.

Reporters clamored for information, and we wondered if this was just a slow news day, or was our story today's breaking news. All we knew was that we were no longer alone. The world would soon hear our sad little story.

Susan Morse, disability advocate, had kicked into gear, and the story of Christopher's crossing was going to make international news.

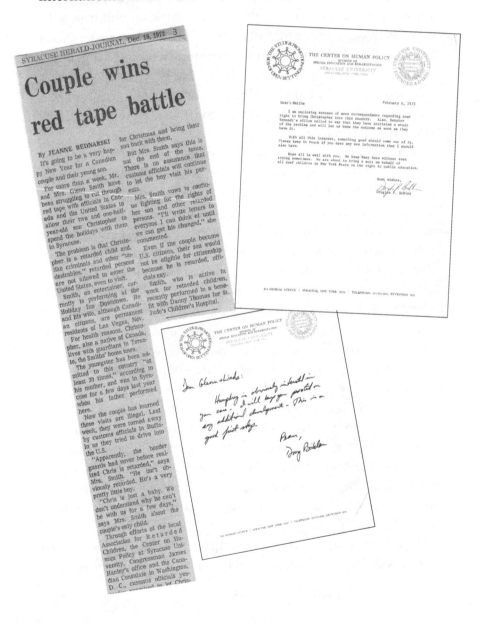

Couple wins red tape battle

By JEANNE BEDNARSKI

It's going to be a very happy New Year for a Canadian couple and their young son.

For more than a week, Mr. and Mrs. Glenn Smith have been struggling to cut through red tape with officials in Canada and the United States to allow their two and one-half-year-old son Christopher to spend the holidays with them in Syracuse.

The problem is that Christopher is a retarded child and, like criminals and other "undesirables," retarded persons are not allowed to enter the United States, even to visit.

Smith, an entertainer, currently is performing at the Holiday Inn Downtown. He and his wife, although Canadian citizens, are permanent residents of Las Vegas, Nev.

For health reasons, Christopher, also a native of Canada, lives with guardians in Toronto, the Smiths' home town.

The youngster has been admitted to this country "at least 20 times," according to his mother, and was in Syracuse for a few days last year when his father performed here.

Now the couple has learned these visits are illegal. Last week, they were turned away by customs officials in Buffalo as they tried to drive into the U.S.

"Apparently, the border guards had never before realized Chris is retarded," says Mrs. Smith. "He isn't obviously retarded. He's a very pretty little boy.

"Chris is just a baby. We don't understand why he can't be with us for a few days," says Mrs. Smith about the couple's only child.

Through efforts of the local Association for Retarded Children, the Center on Human Policy at Syracuse University, Congressman James Hanley's office and the Canadian Consulate in Washington, D. C., customs officials yes- [...]

for Christmas and bring their son back with them.

But Mrs. Smith says this is not the end of the issue. There is no assurance that customs officials will continue to let the boy visit his parents.

Mrs. Smith vows to continue fighting for the rights of her son and other retarded persons. "I'll write letters to everyone I can think of until we can get his changed," she commented.

Even if the couple became U.S. citizens, their son would not be eligible for citizenship because he is retarded, officials say.

Smith, who is active in work for retarded children, recently performed in a benefit with Danny Thomas for St. Jude's Children's Hospital.

THE CENTER ON HUMAN POLICY
DIVISION OF
SPECIAL EDUCATION AND REHABILITATION
SYRACUSE UNIVERSITY

Dear Smiths   February 8, 1973

I am enclosing amounts of more correspondence regarding your right to bring Christopher into this country. Also, Senator Kennedy's office called to say that they have initiated a study of the problem and will let us know the outcome as soon as they have it.

With all this interest, something good should come out of it. Please keep in touch if you have any new information that I should also have.

Hope all is well with you. We keep busy here without even trying sometimes. We are about to bring a suit on behalf of all deaf children in New York State on the right to public education.

Best wishes,

Douglas P. Biklen

THE CENTER ON HUMAN POLICY
SPECIAL EDUCATION AND REHABILITATION
SYRACUSE UNIVERSITY

Dear Glenn + Linda:

Humphrey is obviously interested in your case. I will keep you posted on any additional development. This is a good first step.

Peace,

Doug Biklen

CHAPTER THIRTY

THE INDIAN CHIEF ADOPTION

Zowie! They could go get Chris and bring him to us.

Glenn and I were up all night on an emotional rollercoaster and a whirlwind of activity since the media barged into our room.

The news outlets couldn't get enough of the unfolding story of a family's simple wish to have their child with them for Christmas.

They shot footage of a framed picture of Christopher and of our tiny Christmas tree from every angle, and then stayed to film Glenn's performance.

The result was that the public was outraged by the news report, and we were overwhelmed by a slew of incoming calls all night.

The hotel switchboard was on overload, and at about 2 a.m. we asked them to hold all calls unless it was family or the President of the United States. Chris, of course, was sleeping soundly a few hundred miles away, blissfully unaware of the maelstrom created by his rejection at the border.

The Den of the Little Foxes, where Glenn was performing, was up a flight of stairs from our own hotel room on the twentieth floor. There, the Foxes, (the venue's version of the Playboy Bunnies), were literally hopping mad after hearing the news. After the show they met and formulated a plan.

These young ladies, who had cuddled Chris when Glenn appeared there the year before, loved our little boy. At midnight on Christmas Eve, they came to see us with an offer of help.

These beautiful, hardworking young women would drive to the border at the light of day. They would rent a multi-passenger van that they could all fit in. They would cross the border on a ruse to see the Canadian side of the Falls, and once there they would pick Chris up and smuggle him across the border into the U.S. while distracting the guards with their many assets.

It was quite a picture—a van full of Foxes with Chris bundled up in the middle. They had collected all their tips that night, and they would forfeit their own holiday plans in order to reunite us with our son.

We were grateful to them all. These young women who worked hard to put money on the table for their own families were now pooling their cash to help our family.

Not wanting to risk further ire from the border patrol, we politely declined their kind offer, but not before considering the fun Christopher would have had.

The following day, I was making plans to fly to Toronto, leaving Glenn behind to finish the contract, when there was a knock on the door. It was Christmas day, and after the surprise visit by the media the night before and the bevy of Foxes well into the night, I opened the door with trepidation.

There stood eight American Indians, members of the Onondaga tribe, who had big welcoming smiles on their faces.

With hat in hand, the chief introduced the group, explaining they were there representing their tribal members.

Curious, we invited them in.

It turned out, they had watched the news coverage of our plight last night, and this morning they had convened an emergency meeting of their Grand Council to discuss what they could do to help. Together with their fellow tribesmen, they had developed a plan and they were here to disclose it.

The indian chief adoption

The Onondaga people were one of the original members of the Iroquois Confederacy in northeast North America. Their homeland was in and around present-day Onondaga County, in upstate New York. Our hotel was in Syracuse, which was also in Onondaga County.

We couldn't believe the incongruous assemblage of people. First there had been a ton of media, then a bevy of Foxes, and now the Onondaga Indian chieftain and seven of his tribe members were piled into our already full hotel room containing one bed, two chairs, a desk, and an empty baby bed. The room felt closed in and confining.

Clearing his throat, the chief started.

"Our council members met this morning, and we are here to bring you the good news that was decided upon at this meeting," he solemnly stated.

We were anxious to hear what they had to say.

"As members of the Onondaga Indian tribe, we are citizens of North America. That means we can travel back and forth across the border at will."

Zowie! They could go get Chris and bring him to us.

What came next was not at all what we expected.

"We would like to adopt your son."

What?

The chief continued to share the plan.

"Once the adoption is formalized, Christopher will become a member of our tribe, and he will no longer need a special visa. He will become an Iroquois member, and he will never have to suffer the indignity that has been visited upon him again. We would be honored to adopt your son."

Glenn and I stood there in the ensuing stillness unsure of what to say. These sweet people were serious. They understood discrimination. They had dealt with it their entire lives. Their history was fraught with injustices. They were on a mission of peace and love to try to make up for what had recently happened to our family.

163

"We recognize of course, that this is an unusual idea and fraught with interpretation, but we are merely suggesting that a formal adoption into our tribe will give both him and you the unobstructed freedom to travel across borders as he deserves. He would remain your son, of course, just ours on paper."

What does one say in a situation like this?

Glenn and I looked at each other and said, "Well. . .we kinda like this guy and plan on keeping him, but thank you very much."

CHAPTER \ THIRTY-ONE

A HERO COMES ALONG

If the President of the United States wouldn't help,
who would?

One of the many visitors who knocked on our hotel room door during the holiday week was researcher, teacher, mentor, and all-around good guy, Doug Biklen, who introduced himself as the founding faculty member for the Center on Human Policy at Syracuse University.

Biklin arrived at our hotel room looking like a young Albert Einstein. Intense and serious, with a big mop of wild hair, this earnest gentleman sat on the edge of our bed and explained the mission of his agency.

It must be noted, that our room had just been visited by a psychic who proclaimed Christopher's future as a famous politician. You can't make this stuff up.

The Center on Human Policy (CHP) advocated for the rights of people with disabilities locally, nationally, and globally, and facilitated a critical examination of disability as an aspect of diversity in society. Luckily for us, their office was just down the street from our hotel.

The CHP was founded in 1971, just a few months after Chris' birth, in response to widespread abuse of and discrimination against people with disabilities. Through its programs and activities, the CHP, continuously strived to promote full community participation for all people with disabilities. We were just the kind of cause the fledgling advocacy group was interested in representing.

After several hours taking down all the information we could remember, Doug jumped up from his seat on the end of the bed, promising to go directly to President Nixon and get a pardon for Chris.

He wasn't joking. Doug was angry, and on an urgent mission to right the wrongs that had been visited upon our family. As he took his leave, he turned and said, "I will not rest until Christopher is allowed legal status into this country, you have my word."

Alone again, Glenn and I considered the options that had been presented to us in a short day-and-a-half.

There were cocktail waitresses willing to smuggle our son into the U.S.; an Indian tribe who offered to adopt him; and now an intense young fellow hell-bent on having President Nixon pardon our baby. It was all so crazy. We thought Doug Biklen was a nice guy, but he seemed the most unlikely advocate you could hope to find to carry our message to the White House.

While Doug Biklen, the Onondaga Indian Tribe, the Foxes, the Syracuse ARC, the psychic, the Syracuse Chiefs baseball team, who had jumped into the fray, and hundreds more were trying to find a solution, we were conducting our own research.

A hero comes along

With so much happening in Syracuse in support of our cause, we were becoming more and more optimistic that a solution was in the works, and that we were days away from being able to formalize Christopher's legal entry into the United States.

When we contacted our Canadian immigration attorney to tell him the whole story and get his take on what to do, we were completely taken aback when he said that in researching the laws regarding immigration into Canada by people with disabilities, he came across this terminology:

"People exempt from entering Canada as permanent residents are number one; morons, imbeciles, lunatics, and idiots, and their families; number two, criminals."

At the turn of the century, "imbecile" was the term used for developmentally delayed, while a "moral imbecile" suffered from a form of mental deviance or insanity.

In 1910, Canadian law considered both "imbeciles" and "insane persons" as inadmissible classes. This language had never been challenged.

Our attorney was in a state of shock on finding this language on the books in his beloved country. When considering discrimination in immigration history, scholars tended to concentrate on race and ethnicity, with occasional reference to physical disability.

This traditional focus eclipsed the legacy of systemic discrimination experienced by persons with mental disabilities under Canadian and U.S. immigration laws. Examination of early immigration statutes exposes how North America's immigration regime had historically perceived immigrants with mental disabilities as deviant and defective.

Disability advocate Jean Vanier stated, "In society, the person with an intellectual disability is still too often rejected and despised. Despite the tremendous progress that has been made in terms of integration in schools and the workplace, we still often see today a great ambivalence in the welcome given to people marginalized by intellectual disabilities."

As I contemplated a world of legal discrimination that I knew nothing about until our child was refused entry into the United States, I came to believe that perhaps this challenge was put in front of me for a reason. This was a bigger issue than just our child. What could be done to make people aware of the injustices meted out for so long?

Perhaps when our situation was solved and Chris was firmly ensconced in his home in Las Vegas, I would start a campaign to make people aware of these archaic immigration laws. Perhaps this was my purpose in life. I could visit legislators and change the laws. I could shout from the highest mountains, march with banners held aloft.

Two days after the flurry of activity and assurances from family that Christopher wasn't missing us a bit and was being spoiled by various aunts, uncles, and cousins, things seemed to slow down until we received a call from Doug, excitedly exclaiming that eighty thousand signatures had been gathered and put in front of President Nixon. With this kind of support, our son would surely be traveling with us soon.

But the following day brought bad news. President Nixon turned down the request. We were back at square one.

If the President of the United States wouldn't help, who would?

That day and the next few became a blur as phone calls were exchanged with politicians and celebrities across the U.S. and Canada.

Thanks to the many efforts of Doug Biklen, the University of Syracuse, and the Center on Human Policy, a special man, our hero, Hubert Horatio Humphrey, Jr., the 38th Vice President of the United States, agreed to become Christopher's sponsor.

We were elated. Champagne corks were popped at the Den of the Little Foxes, in Las Vegas, and in our family homes in the U.S. and Canada. We would not have to find ways to smuggle our son into the country. He would not have to be adopted by our Onondaga Indian tribe friends.

We could now legally bring Chris into the country.

Hubert Humphrey remained Christopher's sponsor until the day he died of cancer in 1978 at 66 years of age. For those five years, we religiously renewed his visa every six months.

A month after our champion died, we received a notice that Christopher had to leave the country. Until the laws were changed, it was unlikely that he would be allowed to enter the United States without a sponsor.

That day we knew we could never take him back to visit his Canadian family, nor could we take him to England to visit his British family. He would remain in his Las Vegas home with his parents. We were now officially harboring an illegal alien in the U.S.

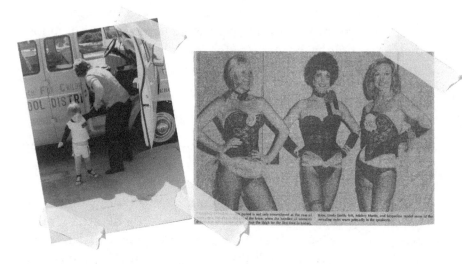

CHAPTER THIRTY-TWO

LAS VEGAS CALLING

There was no denying his "Down syndrome-ness."

Once we realized we could no longer travel as we had done in the past, we decided to put down permanent roots in the U.S. Glenn would still travel, but I would stay in Las Vegas with our son. Chris was now old enough to go to school, and fortunately, it was the law that every child living in the U.S. would receive an education.

Getting Chris enrolled in school was a lengthy process, but the question of his being a legal resident never came up. What was discussed was whether his disability deemed him eligible for special education.

I met with the Clark County School District in Las Vegas, which subsequently conducted a routine assessment of Chris before he could ride on the special bus proudly emblazoned with the proclamation: "Disabled On Board." I didn't think

Chris had a learning disability; I knew he had one. I just wanted to get on with it, but they weren't convinced.

After a month of filing paperwork, meeting with school district officials, psychiatrists, the admissions committee, special education staffers, and more, Chris and I were finally ushered into a room where a panel of eight Clark County educators gravely gazed down the table at me. The diagnosis was in.

"He has Down syndrome," one of the group proudly read to me.

Duh.

Now, I know my son was a cute little guy, but there was no denying his "Down syndrome-ness." His slanted simian eyes were unmistakable; his goofy, loopy walk declared his oddness at hello; his inability to talk; and his fixation on the little white sock (his security blanket replacement sock that he twirled constantly in front of his face making his eyes cross), all certainly shouted NOT NORMAL.

"Therefore, he can't attend mainstream education programs or the school in your neighborhood as they do not have a special education program. He will need to go to Variety School for the Disabled."

Thus, he was consigned to special education classes for the rest of his life. It's not so special to be special.

Months later, I stood at the door waiting for the paratransit bus to pick my little peanut up and take him to his first day at school. Like all mothers of disabled children, I couldn't help but reflect on the journey so far.

Christopher had defied the doctors' orders and lived.

Miraculously, the holes in his heart had closed without the need for surgery. He escaped the one-in-three chance of a childhood cancer sentence. Although not a candidate for legal residency yet, he had a former Vice President of the United States as a sponsor, and he could stay in the U.S. on six-month visas until his legal status was amended.

As the bus pulled up in front of the house, a lump formed in my throat. My five-year-old with an intellect of a much younger child was about to embark on a lifetime of riding in special education transportation. But this was inconsequential to him as he ran toward the bus with his uneven gait, lunch pack dropping to the ground as he held his chubby hands out to the driver.

I sniffled as tears threatened. Chris was our angel, a perfect nonjudgmental child who loved and hugged unabashedly. His early diagnosis of impending death had caused us not to plan too far into the future, but now he left the house an independent little guy.

Among the many issues related to the diagnosis, Down syndrome people were known to be stubborn. This was a big problem because I was stubborn, and so my son had inherited a double dose of stubbornness. Getting him toilet trained was a four-year process. Crawling never happened, no matter how many examples were given, however butt-scooting was effective.

Walking came slow, which caused him to be behind kids his own age by several years. When Chris was a toddler, and he started walking, he refused to step over a crack in the sidewalk. This obviously created many frustrations, as we hoisted him out of harm's way.

On the other hand, he could swim at two, read eighty words and understand their meaning, and he could play the piano—not recognizable tunes, but melodic tinkling nonetheless.

Christopher's early years were fraught with failures and triumphs—success when he put his shoe on the right foot and failure when he refused to verbally communicate.

He called me Ninya and sometimes Mom; his other spoken words were "Chris" and "no." That was it, except for "Aww shit."

His intractability caused him to disregard any enticements. He simply wasn't interested.

In addition to mental retardation, Down syndrome entailed heart defects in about forty percent of cases, (yes, Chris had that); poor muscle tone (that too); plus, loose joints (oh yeah); and a malformed digestive tract (which would rear its ugly head in his twenties); the possibility of childhood cancer (dodged that bullet); early-onset Alzheimer's disease (he had that); short stature (yep); obesity (no); hearing and vision problems (yep); and immune deficiencies (certainly).

People like my Christopher were the bravest people around, overcoming obstacles that would bring most of us to our knees.

His stubborn streak and obsessive-compulsive disorders, which were also a common trait of people with Down syndrome, would hold him back throughout his life.

He would never understand the consequences of his actions no matter how hard we tried to point them out. In later years, we found that Chris also had autism, another consequence of his "Down syndrome-ness."

And yet, my little peanut was like every other five-year-old who went to school and embarked on his own path. I wished his teachers luck.

Christopher thrived at Variety School in Las Vegas. As a way to say thank you to the country that paid our wages and provided an education for our son, Glenn and I continued to perform in and produce a fundraiser we started in Canada when Chris was first born. We called the event "The Concert of Love," and over the years it raised millions of dollars for the disabled.

I was introduced to a small, struggling organization called Opportunity Village that helped disabled adults after I received a call from Joylin Vandenberg, one of the founders of the nonprofit. Joylin had toiled for years to try and gain support from an uncaring community after she gave birth to her own disabled daughter.

After she heard about our Canadian/U.S. border incident, and learned that we lived in Las Vegas, Joylin reached out to see if this peripatetic entertainer couple had been asked to support any local charities. Surely we wanted to support the community, didn't we? And given that our child was disabled, what better cause to join than hers?

Joylin, who was charming and lovely, suggested a tour of Opportunity Village. She also belonged to the Vanguards, a group of volunteer women, and she was amused to hear I had volunteered at their thrift store while pregnant with Christopher.

Within this group was an impressive mix of celebrity wives, often entertainers themselves, whose husbands headlined on the Strip. These women banded together and created an annual "Celebrity Wives Fashion Show."

They found clothing donors from high-end retail shops, raided their own closets, and enlisted their celebrity friends as models. They choreographed, produced, and directed the event and then sold the clothes and accessories to a show-room full of eager bargain hunters, with the proceeds going to Opportunity Village. It was glamourous work, and my first foray into the unique nonprofit arena in Las Vegas.

I soon became immersed in volunteer fundraising for the disabled. I licked envelopes, and called for and retrieved donated goods. My new little home became Charity Head-quarters.

I wasn't the only celebrity wife with a disabled child. More than a few of the well-known people in this group had chil-dren with disabilities, though they wouldn't admit it, which was a mystery to me. I can only surmise their reluctance was due to the stigma attached. Sadly, it continues today.

As a young mom of a profoundly disabled child, I wanted people to notice my kid. He was cool and his life had value, and I felt a responsibility to make people understand that value. Not just for Chris, but for the millions like him. Christopher was not his diagnosis; he had unique and extraordinary gifts to share. His capacity to love and ask for nothing in return was a lesson for all of us.

If I could make people care, everyone would benefit because I felt it was more important to care than to be liked. I wanted to live in a caring community.

My forays into the nonprofit arena through the celebrity world proved to be a great distraction from the tremendous responsibility of caring for Chris. Those were fun times, and I learned the ins and outs of fundraising.

Glenn was a part of this community also, performing often at many of the local galas, particularly when called upon by our friend, Wayne Newton.

Most charity leaders in town knew Glenn could always be counted on to help. Entertaining was one of the ways we could give back to our community. But I was starting to see that the generosity of the attendees didn't always go to the charity.

I was often surprised to learn how much of the money raised was used to fund the event. The hotels, the unions, the party planners, and everyone else got their cut. This didn't make sense to me. If an entertainer was willing to perform at no cost, why couldn't all the others donate their time and resources? Surely the donors wanted to see their money go directly to the cause.

I was shocked and dismayed by what I saw when I took a tour of Opportunity Village that operated out of a small warehouse in an industrial part of town.

Here were these disabled adults, these beautiful, welcoming, innocent souls, clumped together in a dimly-lit warehouse that was cold in the winter and hot in the summer.

Seated at long tables, they worked on a contract for a local restaurant chain, placing packaged plastic knives, forks, and spoons in small white sleeves. They received a paycheck based on the number of units they assembled. Others sorted decks of cards and crayons. It was mundane repetitive work.

It was so discouraging that I wanted to grab them all and run like hell. It certainly wasn't a place or an organization I wanted my son to be a part of.

After the visit, I sat in my car and cried.

But once I got home and protectively hugged Christopher ever closer, what I remembered most about my visit were the hugs and the welcoming smiles of all the occupants. They found joy in the camaraderie and acceptance of their peers, and in performing the simplest of tasks. They were taking part in their version of the American dream. They had a job.

Those were the ingredients for giving disabled people a real life and a real purpose, but I wondered what could be done to improve the recipe. That was when I found my Las Vegas calling, except I wouldn't be able to answer that call until I resolved the past.

CHAPTER THIRTY-THREE

Child abuse victims ask for approval of stiff protection act

CHILD PROTECTION ACT

My last court date more than twenty years ago resulted in an acquittal for my father.

After moving permanently to Las Vegas, I became a full-time volunteer for the disabled community, choosing not just Special Olympics and Opportunity Village, but the Muscular Dystrophy Association, The Down Syndrome Organization, and the Celebrity Wives group.

At the time, OV operated a small, volunteer-run, retail "celebrity boutique" downtown on Main Street adjacent to their larger thrift store. The boutique enjoyed a reputation across the country as the place to shop for celebrity duds while in Las Vegas.

Taxi cabs and limos would pull up, and I remember seeing Gladys Knight and her mother shopping and donating regularly alongside local Strip entertainers.

One day, comedians Belle Barth and Totie Fields came through the door together to drop off a donation of designer clothing that had been tailored for their ample bodies. They regaled all in the store with their ribald humor. They were regular visitors along with local comedian Cork Proctor, who would often grab the store's intercom system and do his Las Vegas act for our customers. With Cork, Belle, and Totie in the store at the same time, there was little business conducted, but lots of laughter, with the sincerest laughs coming from our own disabled folks. When Cork Proctor married local PR icon Carolyn Hamilton, the star-crossed lovers turned their celebrity wedding into a benefit for Opportunity Village.

While engaged in fundraising and volunteerism, I met a group of women active in child welfare, The Medical Wives Society. They soon extracted stories from me about my sordid childhood and journey from England to Canada to Las Vegas. They were very interested in what I went through for a specific reason.

In the mid-1980s, Nevada's laws pertaining to child welfare were antiquated, discriminatory, and needed to be updated. Testimonies were required from credible people, and there were few who would come forward. And so that's how I came to testify on behalf of Nevada's neglected and abused children the following week at an upcoming legislative session in Carson City, Nevada for the Nevada Child Protection Act.

I had not expected to revisit this ugly time in my life and had moved on, but I was dismayed to hear of the abusive system that still existed and agreed to testify on the condition that my identity not be revealed. I didn't want to do anything that would embarrass my family, especially my mother. Nor was I willing to confuse a community, which had very little information about my past—how could Linda Smith, disability advocate, also be a victim of child abuse?

Flying into Carson City, I had second thoughts. My last court date more than twenty years earlier had resulted in an acquittal for my father. He was a child molester, a wife beater, and con-man, yet somehow, even after the agonizing statements given by his own children of the disgusting things he did to them, the court had decided that he was the victim. I didn't have much faith in the system.

The day I was scheduled to testify in Carson City, the room was packed, and the balcony was filled with adolescents and educators on a school field trip. When I was called, I walked to the podium and nervously stated my name and occupation to a surprised group of legislators, many who were my friends, who wondered why Linda Smith, a disability activist, was here today when the subject was child abuse.

It was disconcerting to think that the young people in the balcony would also hear my words. I couldn't help but wonder, given the statistics on child abuse, how many of them may have suffered as I did, and if they would be negatively impacted by the story I was about to tell.

Speaking softly, I told the awful story, describing in detail my sordid childhood—a memory I had long repressed—the police interrogation room, and the theft of innocence a second time by a system that was supposed to protect the innocent. I spoke about the humiliation I suffered as a young child who was forced to describe specific and personal details to a cold and indifferent group of uniformed men.

It was evident that the faces surrounding me registered shock and dismay at hearing my story. Ashamed and embarrassed, I struggled on. This was the first time I had publicly acknowledged the brutality of my early life. It had taken several years into my marriage before I even told Glenn about my upbringing, painting a picture that explained my poor sister's erratic behavior. It was only when he expressed instant understanding and acceptance of Jean's plight that I tentatively told him about my own abuse.

I continued to tell my story to a rapt audience.

Once my father was deported from Canada, we changed our names and soldiered on with a plan to put the past behind us. In the end, our story of abuse was so improbable that even the courts refused to believe us. It wasn't until my father, who planned to kill us, was caught with a gun, that he was finally deported from Canada back to England.

We later learned that he continued his abusive ways after he returned home. I was nearly thirty when I found out I had a half-sister in England. She had reached out to Terry, to tell him of her own abuse by this man. Our father, the destroyer of children, the annihilator of dreams had continued to wreak havoc a continent away.

I ended my testimony with a request to change the system, most importantly the handling and processing of children who were victims of incest and abuse.

In this country, more than three million children are victimized by sexual predators every year. An equal number of cases go unreported. Most often children are abused by someone they love and trust, and they are victimized a second time in the retelling of their stories. Nevada's method of interviewing children who had suffered abuse was no different. Not much had changed over the years.

The hoped-for new laws would include gender-appropriate counselors, rooms painted in hues of soft pinks and blues designed to welcome children, and anatomically correct dolls that would assist the children in describing what they had endured. I asked them to pass the entire bill so that innocent children would not have to suffer the humiliation that I had endured.

I said, "Children need and deserve trained advocates and a foolproof system in place to protect them in order to shield them from the cruelties they never should have to experience in life."

Then I turned and walked away, choking back tears, head down. People could be heard weeping. In the balcony the kids applauded.

My testimony that day evoked a media frenzy with headlines that noted the emotional statement of a prominent community member who wished to remain anonymous, and the passing of new laws to replace the existing archaic child protection laws.

The Nevada Child Protection Bill passed unanimously in 1989, and I was credited with changing laws that would protect Nevada children. I left Carson City feeling vindicated for all I had endured as a child.

Testifying in front of the committee and sharing this story in such a public way turned out to be a cathartic cleansing of my soul, an acceptance of "Linda the child" who was now a warrior for helpless children. The experience also opened me up to ask myself all kinds of questions about my past, questions about my life before I became the mother of a child with a disability.

Did my past strengthen me? Did it prepare me for the birth of my disabled son? Did it propel me forward in a quest to right wrongs? What was driving me? How was this battered child and homeless teen able to convince mega stars and casino moguls to come together in a Concert of Love?

I was often plagued by doubt and distrust in my own abilities and motives. I always questioned my purpose on earth. Some people say our paths are chosen for us.

Maybe that was true.

CHAPTER THIRTY-FOUR

SPECIAL OLYMPICS BENEFIT — Athletic programs for the handicapped throughout Nevada will benefit from the Rogers Celebrity Concert scheduled for 3 p.m. in the Aladdin Theatre of Performing Arts. Aladdin General Manager Ed Nigro, seated, discussed the final seating plans for the event with chairwoman Linda Smith, right. Also pictured are volunteer Debbie Tubbs and Aladdin entertainment executive Peter Anthony.

THE ALADDIN

I had my work cut out for me.

My life had new purpose I had found a challenge I could sink my teeth into. I would work to get these special souls out of that dreadful place. I would make my mark on the town and improve the lot for these special needs kids. I just wasn't sure how to go about it.

The good news was I had some background working with charities for the disabled. In the early 1980s, I was asked to serve on the Board of Special Olympics. Serving on this International Board meant that I met people of influence, people who could assist me with my dream of a fabulous place for the Opportunity Village or "OV" folks.

The Special Olympics' mission was one that I could really get excited about, and I set out to make a difference for this cause. I would produce a charity concert.

At the time, Glenn was recording with Gladys Knight in Nashville, and the same month he appeared in the Congo showroom at the Sahara Hotel with Don Rickles. Those were glamorous and exciting times. Glenn was in an enviable position to solicit the support of those two well-known celebrities, who I felt certain could be counted on to perform in the concert.

But to really sell it, I was hoping to get Kenny Rogers, who had just released his latest hit single "Lady." Kenny was appearing in the Golden Nugget lounge in downtown Las Vegas and with the chart-topping success of "Lady" I was certain he was looking for more prestigious bookings.

I put together a plan that would make Kenny the hero for Special Olympics. Being overly optimistic, I had no trouble imagining the moon and the stars, and without permission from Kenny or his ensemble, I went to the Aladdin Theatre for the Performing Arts on the famed Las Vegas Strip to negotiate his performance in a benefit concert.

Outside of the main showrooms on the Strip, the Aladdin sported the only concert venue in Nevada with a grand 7,000-seat theater, the largest performance center in town. My good friend Debbie Jackson worked there, and she was able to open the door for me to meet with the hotel's executives.

The Aladdin, however, had a history that was plagued with rumors of racism, theft, kickbacks, income tax fraud and evasion. A recent $50 million expansion that included a 700-room tower and new Theatre for the Performing Arts was the beginning of the hotel's financial problems and allegations of mob control.

Undoubtedly, the Aladdin was in need of some good press. The hotel, which had changed hands many times, lost money each year. Even the wedding of the King of Rock and Roll, Elvis Presley, to Priscilla Beaulieu at the hotel didn't help its bottom line. But hosting a charitable concert would bring badly needed goodwill and PR. I decided they needed me.

The aladdin

The pitch was to help the hotel by bringing thousands of guests to their venue. Concert guests would fill the theater in support of Special Olympics. All the hotel had to do was allow the use of the theater at no cost.

Using Kenny Rogers' name to gain access, my appointment with the Entertainment Director at the Aladdin was easily arranged. I didn't know Kenny Rogers at that time, but it was just a teeny untruth for a good cause.

Sitting across from the smartly dressed executive, I laid out my plan for a large concert with an appearance by a mega superstar by the name of Kenny Rogers who was certain to pack the house at no cost to the hotel. Why wouldn't it. This was a prestigious venue and more celebrities would be certain to join in. It was a great charitable cause with all proceeds going to Special Olympics.

What could be better?

Confident about the outcome, I said it was a win/win proposition for all parties involved.

"I am respectfully asking the Aladdin to donate the use of its beautiful, acoustically perfect Theater for the Performing Arts. The stagehands' union, musicians' union, and the culinary union will donate their time as well. In addition to the theater, the hotel could kindly throw in the showroom technicians, including a full complement of theater staff."

Pausing for a millisecond, I said, "It would be terrific to have a few suites for the celebrities to lounge in as they prepare for their appearance. Food and drink would also need to be donated for the green room, various dressing rooms, and after party. Could your catering department put something special together for approximately fifty people? And perhaps some sweet rolls and coffee for the musicians and handlers?"

I rattled on: "What you will get is a hotel full of celebrities, for free, and an event that will be the talk of the town. Headliners like Wayne Newton, Gladys Knight and the Pips, and Don Rickles. Heck, I could also get the showgirls in the

Follies Bergere to greet the arriving guests in the lobby. As you know, the celebrities mentioned are each contracted for large fees in other casino properties around town, but I will bring them here to your place of business at no cost to you."

Sucking in the last remaining air in the room, I plowed on.

"It would be a major coup for the Aladdin, as you will be the first on the Strip to showcase Kenny Rogers. I guarantee members of the Kennedy family will come since Eunice Kennedy Shriver is the founder of Special Olympics, and Arnold Schwarzenegger will come because he's dating Maria Shriver, a longtime advocate for children's health and disability issues. We can host them for an after party!

"Best of all, the Aladdin will benefit from 7,000 or more attendees at your property on a Sunday afternoon. There will be guaranteed casino play. The dining rooms will enjoy abundant traffic, and the hotel will be full of spenders."

Having thrown in all the best bits, all that was needed was a yes. Of course, I didn't have a celebrity signed on yet, but I knew that once I signed the theater, I could get Kenny Rogers and his management team to agree to this one-time charitable performance.

The Concert of Love would prove to be a wonderful comeback occasion for Kenny and a great venue to announce his move from a small lounge downtown to the largest venue on the Strip. And, he would be a hero for supporting an internationally-recognized charity and the biggest fundraising event Las Vegas had ever seen. I had it all figured out.

After listening to my plan, the entertainment director thought for a moment. Then he looked at me and said, "Certainly not." And he threw me out of his office.

CHAPTER THIRTY-FIVE

June 30, 1980

Mrs. Linda Smith
c/o Nevada Special Olympics
900 East Karen Avenue
Suite H-214
Las Vegas, NV 89109

Dear Linda:

Thank you so much for your kindnesses to Maria and me during our visit to Las Vegas. How lucky Special Olympics is to have you. You are so creative, charming and enthusiastic -- and so is that wonderful husband of yours!

I expect Special Olympics in Las Vegas to be one of the best programs. I have watched your program with great interest in the last couple of years. If there are any ways in which the National Office can be of help in terms of training families or parents, or brothers and sisters, let me know, or give me a call here at my office. Training children is one of my major interests -- it is the heart of the Special Olympics program because it makes children feel confident and full of joy, and thereby similar emotions are passed along among the parents.

Please keep in touch. Thanks again for a wonderful visit.

Sincerely,

Eunice K Shriver

Eunice Kennedy Shriver

PEBBLE IN THE LAKE

I finally ran out of air and ideas and shut up.

WHAT?

I was stunned.

Did he not hear what I was offering? What part of "I am bringing a passel of celebrities and thousands of people to your doorstep" did he not hear? This simply couldn't be!

But there I was, summarily dismissed, outside in the cold.

My head was spinning. Befuddled, but not yet defeated, I walked slowly down the hall, passing the executive suites of the hotel, already strategizing my next move. I needed to get another appointment and make my pitch to someone smarter than this last guy.

Maybe he would see me now?

As luck would have it, there was a light at the end of the hall, a rainbow of many colors—an open door. Not just any door, not just any office—this was the big one—the golden-etched plaque spelled the hotel president's name, an open door beckoned me to walk into its sanctuary.

Peering into an empty outer office, I saw an open invitation to enter.

What was the worst that could happen? I'd be thrown out again?

I barged in and found a secretary engrossed in conversation with the man himself at the entry to another, larger office. A voice in my head said, *Don't stop now.*

"Hi, I'm Linda Smith. I just met with your entertainment director. . . sorry for barging in. . ., but I saw your open door and wanted to introduce myself and say thank you for all you do to make Las Vegas the entertainment capital of the world. Your hotel is spectacular—a fabulous place! I wanted to take this opportunity to tell you in person how amazing your staff is. I knew you would appreciate that. I am certain you hear it every day, but I wanted to add my voice, and let you know that they have been so kind and welcoming to me. I am so very impressed and thought you should know."

The hotel president and his secretary stared, mouths open, as I gestured down the hall in the direction of the office from which I had so recently been rudely dismissed.

"Peter and I were just discussing an upcoming celebrity concert headlined by Kenny Rogers, Gladys Knight, and Don Rickles, to name a few. Am I interrupting anything? If it's inconvenient, I can come back some other time."

I paused for a short second, then continued on.

"The concert, which is guaranteed to be sold out, will attract 7,000-plus fans and prominent Las Vegans who will be sure to partake in all that this beautiful hotel has to offer. The concert will be the talk of the town, and your hotel will enjoy full dining rooms plus table and slot play. Perhaps you might be in town to say a few words of welcome from the stage? Lots of media are certain to be in attendance. Oh, and the Kennedy family is expected to attend. I will suggest they stay at your hotel. Perhaps you could donate a few suites for them and host a small reception to follow the concert. . . I will get a photographer to capture some great shots."

A breath, then my best plea,

"My son, Christopher, is in Special Olympics, and his father is appearing with Don Rickles. Did I tell you that a celebrity softball game will take place the day before the Concert? Cher, Kenny, Gladys, and others will play against local and national media, followed by the concert. Do you play softball?"

I finally ran out of air and ideas and shut up.

The secretary, whose mouth was hanging open in a perfect "O," looked at me and then her boss, ready to toss me out as soon as he gave her the nod.

Instead, he looked bemused, accompanied by the softening of his eyes and mouth. It was a look of recognition from one scrapper to another. At this point, I had nothing to lose. I had already received a "no," so what the heck! Besides, "no" to me was simply the start of a negotiation. Who knew what could come of this intrusion?

In the end, providence was on my side. I got the answer I was seeking and sailed out of the hotel triumphant with a "yes." A big "YES." Yes, to everything. I believed this clever man knew a gambler when he saw one, especially one on a winning streak. He wasn't about to break that luck.

I learned a valuable lesson in fundraising that day.

"No"—is just the start of a negotiation. I didn't fully realize it then, but I had thrown a pebble into the open lake, instigating a ripple effect which would set the foundation for the rest of my life. As the hot summer sun pierced through the dancing clouds I skipped down Las Vegas Boulevard.

Once the Aladdin Theatre for the Performing Arts was secured, everything else fell into place. The entertainment director did not hold a grudge against me for going over his head and instead jumped on board to help make the event a success. Kenny's manager understood the showcase this venue would give his client and agreed to his performance as the event headliner. Gladys, Rickles, Wayne, and other Las Vegas legends signed on, too. The unions were all on board with strip musicians and stage technicians donating their services.

The invitation to Eunice Kennedy Shriver was sent, and she agreed to attend along with her daughter, Maria Shriver, and Maria's then boyfriend, Arnold Schwarzenegger. Debbie lined up all the food for the reception, and her mom and sister made the desserts.

Kenny Rogers was still fulfilling his contract downtown at the Golden Nugget, and through his manager, an appointment was made for me to meet with the Nugget's owner, Steve Wynn, who was charming and showed me a mockup of the new hotel he was going to build, The Mirage Hotel. Steve Wynn also donated $20,000 to the cause. This contribution, the first of many, was monumental at the time. The concert raised $100,000 and was a success before it ever took place.

I was on a roll.

CHAPTER THIRTY-SIX

CONCERT OF LOVE

Mr. Las Vegas opened doors.

Glenn and I made our mark on the Las Vegas charity scene by producing and appearing in the annual Concert of Love. This was the successor to the first concert we did that took place in Toronto, Canada shortly after Christopher was born that featured Gilda Radner, Martin Short, and Paul Schaffer.

With a successful event under our belts, we had a formula for success. The way to raise real funds was to find a large venue free of charge, and everything else would fall into place.

Glenn did what he did best and thoroughly entertained the crowd, garnering many standing ovations. The general ticket prices were low so we could fill the room with people delighted to see the inside of a showroom, whereas the expensive seats up front were sold to locals with lots of disposable income.

Wayne Newton, also known as Mr. Las Vegas, was the hottest ticket in town, and we were fortunate to enjoy his friendship. Glenn was a great entertainer, but not a headliner on his own, and it was more than helpful to have Wayne open doors and get the big casino bosses to pay attention.

We were also friends with Walter Kane, the entertainment director for the Howard Hughes properties. At first I sold tickets to the concert by telling people they would get their money back if they didn't like the show, a testament to our conviction that if we could fill the joint, we would win the hearts and pocketbooks of future donors. But in the beginning, ticket sales for the "Glenn Smith Concert of Love" were slow. In a town with more than its share of entertainment options, people weren't sure the concert would be worth their time or money.

Producing a Las Vegas concert was a heady experience, and I needed plenty of help. My friends Dick and Lynn Foster, who owned Foster Productions, directed the concerts and donated their staff all for free for twenty-five years.

Everyone involved was expected to help sell tickets, and as such, I made my way up and down the Las Vegas Strip and downtown haunts, doling out several hundred to every entertainer, enlisting the help of union members, waiters, bartenders, and entertainer friends to get the tickets sold.

On the list were two dynamo local entertainers Jackie and Mollie McCall, identical twins, who played a mean violin and would jump up from the audience and join Glenn on stage from time to time. They were the most connected and energetic people I had ever met. Jackie dated Frank Sinatra, Jr., and Mollie hung out with the Kennedy clan. They were identical in the truest sense of the word, so much so that at times, one would fill in for the other.

To get the tickets sold as expediently as possible, Jackie and Mollie had the idea to enlist Al Bramlet, the head of the

Culinary Union 226, the largest union in town, to sell tickets to its thousands of members, who worked in hospitality, hotel, gaming, food and beverage, service, manufacturing, textile, laundry, distribution, and airport industries. I was elated at the probability of quick sales with Bramlet pushing them into his union members' hands.

Although he was a respected community leader and benefactor to many local charitable endeavors, Bramlet was also rumored to be connected to the underworld.

A problem occurred when the McCall sisters gave 300 tickets to Bramlet's sidekick, the Secretary-Treasurer of Culinary Local 226, to sell. The twins were certain that proceeds from the sale would be in my hands in a few days.

A week passed.

I was concerned, and as the concert date drew close, I called them daily for an update. Each time they contacted their ticket source, he reassured them that the tickets had already been sold, and the money would be in their hands that night. This scene was repeated for several days, and I was anxious to get the funds into the charity's coffers.

New to the Las Vegas scene, I had much to prove. Also as a board member of the beneficiary charity, I didn't want to be seen as irresponsible for giving away 300 tickets.

It was time to visit the man in person and collect the money. The McCall twins assured me that their guy was legit; as a matter of fact, he had come into the showroom nightly to boast how many tickets he had sold and to seek even more to sell. The girls delivered another batch of tickets to his home in a trendy condo complex on Flamingo Road, just steps away from the Las Vegas Strip. I went to that address respectfully dressed. I was a charity lady ready to accept the funds and write the man a receipt.

It was a large, two-story apartment complex in the style of the day with steps up to the second floor where balconies overlooked a sparkling pool and freshly mowed grass.

I knocked on the door and a swarthy, unkempt character peered out at me, glancing past me to see if I was alone.

Immediately alarm bells went off in my head. This guy looked like a mobster straight out of Central Casting. I was already regretting this trip as I stammered on about why I was there.

"Look lady, I don't know what you're talkin' about. I don't know no twin sisters, and I got no money for you. I got more important things to do."

The voice in my head told me to run. . . *Get out of here, Linda. . . now.*

He said it again. "I don't know the people you are looking for or anything about the tickets and charity concerts. . . you got the wrong guy, so shove off."

"But. . ." I spluttered, "Jackie and Mollie said this is the address. Are you with the Culinary Union?"

He glowered as I stood with one foot across the threshold. The foolishness of my trip was sinking in. He could slam the door shut or drag me inside.

My eyes flittered about. My car was in the parking lot, and I considered the number of steps it would take to get to it if I had to run. *Why had I come alone?*

"Lady, get lost." And with that declaration, he slammed the door in my face.

Stunned, I darted down the steps. I knew the guy was lying. The concert was just two days away, and we were facing a venue with 300 empty seats or a full one with a chunk of the money missing.

I made my way to the phone booth adjacent to the pool, and placed a panicked call to Jackie and Mollie blurting out what had just transpired. They said they would be right over.

As I waited for them, I could see the drapes in the man's apartment occasionally part. He was keeping an eye on me and I was keeping an eye on him.

Although three miles away when I called, the McCall twins came barreling around the corner in less than a heartbeat.

Both girls weighed less than a hundred pounds dripping wet, but they bolted up the stairs, two at a time, with a determination that was amazing to behold. The apartment door burst open and my guy flew out, catapulting himself over the balcony and onto the street. He took off running with the girls in hot pursuit. Shocked, I stood there unable to move.

He hoisted himself over a wall, while Jackie easily sprinted over as if she were a track and field star. All of this happened so fast, playing out like a bad action movie. After fifteen minutes, the girls came panting back. He got away, and they knew they had trusted the wrong guy.

When I think back on that day, I can't believe the chances we all took. This was a bad dude, and we were in over our heads. He had taken the money for the tickets he sold and spent it. What a mess. There went my reputation as a competent event producer.

In the end, the McCall sisters hit the town for forty-eight hours, reselling every ticket. Al Bramlet gave us a personal gift and a larger one on behalf of the union. The show was a sell-out and a financial success, and we never heard from the fleeing culinary "business agent" again.

Al Bramlet was a Las Vegas character, who knew the rich and powerful, and became rich and powerful himself. Eventually he apologized for the "miscommunication." All was well in Sin City.

In 1976, Bramlet led a culinary strike that paralyzed the Strip and shut it down. At about the same time, a few independent restaurants tried to decertify the Culinary Union. That's when firebombs were planted at those restaurants, exploding while diners were inside. We suspected our fleeing friend of planting the bombs.

Bramlet denied any union involvement in the bombings in an interview that turned out to be his last. Ten days after the Concert of Love, Bramlet was murdered. He was shot numerous times, stripped of his clothing, and his body was placed under a pile of rocks in the desert. Without a doubt, it was a mob hit. Vegas was run by organized crime, and I wasn't ready for prime-time.

Still, after this almost disastrous learning experience, I was stunned that over a thousand people came to see the Glenn Smith Concert of Love. From auspicious beginnings, a successful annual event was launched in Nevada, a concert that continued to draw sellout crowds for twenty-five years. The 25th Concert of Love starred Celine Dion and raised a million dollars in one day.

Every year a Las Vegas showroom donated the venue. The lighting and sound technicians and celebrities all generously gave their time and talents. Equally unheard of, the musicians' union donated the orchestras.

With celebrities like Tom Jones, Engelbert Humperdinck, Joan Rivers, the rock group Chicago, the Everly Brothers, Ann Margret, Tony Orlando, and, of course, Wayne Newton, the event raised hundreds of millions of dollars over the years for our favorite charity—Opportunity Village.

CHAPTER THIRTY-SEVEN

FULL-TIME FUNDRAISER

*I was flying by the seat of my pants
and making it up along the way.*

Opportunity Village began in 1954 against all odds, when families like mine were told that their kids had no value, no place in society. The story of the organization's origins and those of every other disability organization across the nation was one of perseverance, hope and vision, and of families' love for some of the most undervalued and misunderstood people in the world.

Over the course of history, people with visible differences had been judged as less than human, cast aside at birth, treated as disposable, or imprisoned in facilities built for 300 that instead housed 3,000.

It wasn't until the mid-1960s that children with disabilities were permitted to attend public school. From the very moment of their birth, they were labeled uneducable, unemployable, and unworthy.

Thanks to parent activism, in 1975 The Education for All Handicapped Children Act (EHA) became law. At that time, U.S. public schools accommodated only one out of five children with disabilities, and many states had laws that excluded children with certain types of disabilities from attending public school, including those who were blind, deaf, or labeled "emotionally disturbed" or "mentally retarded."

At the time the EHA was enacted, more than one million children in the U.S. had no access to the public school system. Many of these children lived in state institutions where they received limited or no educational or habilitation services. Another 3.5 million children attended school but were "warehoused" in segregated facilities and received little or no effective instruction.

When I was first introduced to Opportunity Village, it was a small, struggling organization founded by seven families who were told their children were uneducable and unemployable. Wanting nothing more than acceptance for their children, who were denied an education, they formed the Clark County Association for Retarded Citizens (CCARC). They came together much like every disability organization in the country did: with parents' resolve to prove their children had value and much to contribute to society, and like the little engine that could, CCARC prevailed. What started as a school evolved into an employment training center for people with intellectual disabilities.

Respecting their mission, I was recruited onto their board of directors—and quickly realized this charity was in trouble when the first meeting went into its third hour.

The meeting was an after-hours potluck with no formal agenda. Competing conversations were taking place simultaneously. The entire first hour of actual business was spent discussing whether cookies or carrots should be served at the Friday night dances. That was item one out of twenty. It was clear this meeting would not be productive.

As a volunteer and new board member, I became aware of the dire state of the organization's budget and facilities. As a "celebrity wife" and Vanguard Auxiliary member, I was shielded from problems. We helped with events but, were insulated from the harsh reality of the poor facilities and lack of organization.

"Why are we discussing cookies and carrots when the roof is falling in," I asked, pointing to the hole in the ceiling and the bucket below. The building, a former 7-UP bottling plant, was cold and poorly lit. 7-UP had the foresight to move their employees out, so why was it okay for the folks we served to be here?

The building was locked in by Charleston Boulevard and an interstate overpass. If there were an emergency (flooding on Charleston was a common occurrence), everyone would be trapped.

At the conclusion of my third Board meeting, I was asked to take a job as their first fundraiser at an annual salary of $15,000. There was no money to pay my salary, which meant if I wanted to be paid, I would have to earn the money myself. It was my first real job outside of entertaining, and I decided that I would fix that leaky roof! Heck, I *would* get them another building.

Like so many nonprofits of the time, the Board of Directors, was comprised mostly of family members, and was in dire need of business leaders. This reality was tricky to navigate, as the founding families should certainly not be forgotten and in fact should be lauded for their efforts and struggles over the years.

As a mom of a disabled child, I understood what it meant to be alone with your troubles. Our children had been neglected, abused, and maligned. These founding parents had been at it much longer than I had, and most had suffered for years with little or no services for their children.

The most vulnerable amongst us arrived at a dilapidated building each day with a resolve and a smile that would melt even the most cynical hearts. They were not concerned that the location was difficult to get to, or that little was expected of them. Instead, they were grateful every day for the support they were being given.

Surely I could be the champion they needed.

My first year on the job had its ups and downs, and no shortage of fodder for a book about what *not* to do in the business of fundraising! In short, I was flying by the seat of my pants and making it up as I went.

My background proved to be beneficial for the position of lead fundraiser. If I had learned one thing, it was that all things were achievable if you set your sights on the prize. I would focus on the finish line and beyond and not deviate from the plan.

I honed my skills and implemented unconventional methods to draw support for the organization. Although performing an admirable service, Opportunity Village was insulated from the community and was an unknown entity in most Las Vegas households. It needed some good public relations. But there was no money to hire a PR firm, and I was no expert in this area. *Who would want to help?*

I contacted the most respected public relations and media professionals in town, and ask them to serve on a Public Affairs Committee that would meet once a month to offer support and advice. But when I started calling around, I found that they would not take my calls, and their secretaries were declining for them.

I then sent invitations to join "one of the most important Public Information Committees" in Nevada to the heads of all media outlets, including the most beloved on-air personalities of television and radio. The appeal listed all who would be invited to serve. By illustrating the prominence of the invited committee, each person receiving the invitation was flattered they had been asked to join their renowned and distinguished peers. Earl Johnston, editor of the largest newspaper in Nevada, was the first to respond. . . with one condition. The meetings would take place in his boardroom. BINGO.

Others followed suit, not wanting to be the only member of the media not at the table. The result was a 100 percent positive response, just as I had hoped. In the end, we enjoyed the most respected and sought-after volunteer committee in Nevada, if not in the country.

One of the media outlets to join the bandwagon was the *Las Vegas Sun*. This newspaper, owned and operated by Nevada icon Hank Greenspun, quickly took note that the meetings were to be held in their competitor's boardroom. This didn't sit well with the *Sun*'s bellicose executive editor, former Nevada Governor Mike O'Callaghan. He agreed to serve on the committee but wouldn't come to the *Review-Journal* for the meetings. If he was to give his support, then I would go to him. And so I did.

Governor O'Callaghan was a beloved war hero who had received a Bronze Star for valor, but he had paid a high price for his courage. When his company was barraged by heavy artillery from Communist forces during a night attack, Sargent O'Callaghan discovered that soldiers at an outpost had been cut off by enemy action. He voluntarily exposed himself to enemy fire, located his men, and brought them safely back to the trenches. Shortly thereafter, he took a direct hit on the lower leg from an 82-mm mortar round.

"It killed my squad leader, a kid named Johnny Estrada," O'Callaghan recalled forty-six years later. He had rigged a tourniquet out of telephone wire, using a bayonet to twist it tight around his mangled leg.

In addition to being an American hero, Governor O'Callaghan was a hero for Nevada's disenfranchised, including members and families of the disability community. He was an extremely popular governor, who had earned a second term by a four-to-one margin, the greatest landslide in a gubernatorial election in state history. He also had a reputation as a raging bull when provoked or upon hearing of injustices. When he was mad, he was very mad, and it was an unfortunate soul who crossed his path. This man broke every rule in the book regarding human relations. He screamed, he yelled, he cussed you out—he was relentless in his rage.

Despite this fearsome reputation, O'Callaghan was my mentor and I his muse, and we enjoyed a great friendship until his death. He was my personal hero, and I would often go to his office at the newspaper for advice. Sitting across from him at a desk piled so high with paperwork that he could barely see me, I laid the problems out in front of him. He was brilliant, no nonsense, and could always be counted on to help.

One day, I told him about a brewing problem that involved a couple of people to whom he had recommended my charity. I meekly sat as he peered at me over his tower of files, and I told him that two of his friends, former football players who owned McDonald's franchises, had reneged on a commitment to hold a golf tournament to benefit Opportunity Village. After spending months of my time lining up sponsors, including beer and wine distributors, professional volunteers, and a golf course at no cost, these two men changed their choice of charities midstream for one more politically favored by their company.

Since Governor Mike had brokered the deal between the businessmen and Opportunity Village, I was now handing off the problem to him. O'Callaghan asked me why I didn't tell them to shove it. He said if I was going to be in this business, I needed to be more aggressive and tell them in no uncertain terms that changing charity recipients midstream was simply not an option.

I explained that I had attempted to reason with not just them, but with their highly respected PR firm, and that in a face-to-face meeting, they stood towering over me, telling me, "Too bad, lady. It's our event and we have changed the beneficiary charity. It's our prerogative to do so."

This scene with two huge former football players, a local attorney friend, and their PR company rep had played out in my office. I had stood up to the men, but they were bullies who knew they had the upper hand.

The lying duo who had spent their lives charging through the line of scrimmage and trampling over their opponents, were used to getting their way.

As I gulped back tears, Governor Mike said, "Damn it, Smith, I guess I have to solve the problem for you."

This, of course was why I was in his office in the first place.

He picked up the phone, and spent ten minutes berating them, calling them sniveling cowards and more, and generally blasting them without pause for their "chicken-s*** way of conducting business." After hanging up, he turned to me and spit out, "Grow some hair on your ass, Smith" and "Don't take this kind of crap from anyone again."

Well, okay then. This larger than life man had helped pave the way for my success in those early years, so who was I to argue with his style.

My most memorable run-in with Governor O'Callaghan was when I was contacted to bring two disabled citizens to meet the President of the United States at a press conference for Nevada Republican Congressman James Santini, who was running against the Nevada Democratic Senator, Harry Reid.

Sig Rogich was a prominent local ad man heading up the Reagan/Bush campaign. He had ordered 250,000 promotional buttons from the Opportunity Village training center. This unprecedented, historic promotional button order would garner plenty of attention for our organization, and at the same time, people with intellectual disabilities would be in the enviable position of having helped a president get elected.

You could pick our people off the ceiling as they proudly worked around the clock on this contract. Today, if asked who the most important person they ever worked for was, they would sing in unison, *"Elvis Presley, Glenn Smith, Ronald Reagan, and George Bush!"*

Glenn and I were friends with Elvis, and through our friendship we also came to know his longtime manager, Colonel Tom Parker. After enticing him to take a tour of Opportunity Village's small employment center downtown on First Street, the Colonel contracted with OV to make the scarves Elvis wore in his shows each night. The scarves were lovingly made, kissed, packed, and shipped to Elvis wherever he toured.

The Congressman/Senator press event was held in the private Atlantic Aviation airfield hangar on Tropicana Avenue. Representatives of Opportunity Village were supposed to come on stage and present a plaque with the original button for the Reagan/Bush Campaign attached to President Reagan, who we would thank for believing in our abilities and his button order.

Once the OV folks and I were vetted by the Secret Service, we proudly sat in the front row anxiously awaiting a call to the stage. As the paparazzi readied themselves for the big moment, my little group practically levitated off their seats with excitement.

I chose siblings Johnny and Lea to do the honors. Both had intellectual disabilities and were legally blind, and each took part in making the buttons. We practiced the walk onto the stage, the handoff of the plaque, and the words we would speak.

When the moment arrived, instead of being invited onto the stage, a White House staffer grabbed the plaque out of our hands and told us to stay seated. There was a last-minute shuffle, and the plaque was handed to the congressman, who strolled onstage for the photo-op with the president. I was stunned by this development and very disappointed for Johnny and Lea, who had purchased new clothes for the occasion and spent the morning at a hair salon. It was a big deal. We were saddened that we didn't get to make the presentation ourselves, and as bulbs flashed, the congressman thanked the president on behalf of Opportunity Village, and President Reagan looked our way and smiled.

The next day, the *Las Vegas Review-Journal* featured a large photo of the congressman and the president with the caption in large bold type, "Santini thanks President Reagan on Behalf of the Citizens of Opportunity Village."

Reading the paper, the only thing on my mind was how disappointed we were not to have met the president. Otherwise, it was fun to be in such company, and the champagne and hors d'oeuvres were yummy and plentiful.

Then the phone rang. It was my hero, Mike O'Callaghan, who was beyond mad. "How could you let Opportunity Village and the people we serve be used for political purposes?" he bellowed. "Smith, you have singlehandedly lost the election for Harry Reid. If you don't know how to play the game, stay out of the field."

The tirade continued. I was in shock and unable to get a word in. At first, I couldn't comprehend his anger. And then the full import of his words sank in. I had been duped into believing the publicity stunt was about people with disabilities. Instead, it was a political ploy, and we were the pawns.

After squawking at me for an interminable amount of time, he exhausted all expletives and hung up. A few minutes passed, and he called once more to start in again, except this time I refused to take his call. My secretary held the phone out so that I could hear that she was bearing the brunt of his anger.

On the third call, he insisted I talk to him, but by then I was splayed on the floor in a puddle sobbing, and my assistant told him I was unavailable.

After several more calls from him insisting that I get on the phone, I picked it up, feeling angry myself. This time he was to apologize for losing his temper and for taking his frustration out on me.

"It wasn't your fault; it was that jerk Sig Rogich!"

Oh boy. . .Two men I admired so much would now, because of me, be political enemies forever. It turned out that O'Callaghan was correct in his assessment of me. I was naïve.

One week later these two influential men from opposite ends of the political arena were spotted at lunch, the best of friends. Politics does make strange bedfellows.

~~UN~~WANTED

I was a political neophyte, but the lessons I learned about relationship building and navigating through the rough streets of politics, gamblers, the mafia, and more, served my Las Vegas charity work well.

CHAPTER THIRTY-EIGHT

EYES AND EARS BEFORE MOUTH

What if I tripped and fell flat on my face?

In a quest to build Opportunity Village into the most respected and successful organization in Nevada, face-to-face meetings with the most influential and affluent citizens of our community needed to take place.

One memorable meeting was arranged by Governor O'Callaghan. I was to meet E. Parry Thomas, acknowledged in many circles as the most powerful community leader in Las Vegas during the city's formative years.

Not only was Thomas the first banker to issue loans to casino owners, but he also toiled behind the scenes for years to bring in corporations and transform Sin City into something more respectable.

At the time of E. Parry Thomas' arrival in Las Vegas, banks refused to loan money to casinos for two primary reasons.

First, they were concerned about possible ties to organized crime. Second, they were hesitant to loan money to businesses that relied on an element of chance to make a profit. Thomas went against the grain, knowing these businesses were a solid investment.

It was said that Thomas brought the gold to Glitter Gulch, and here I was, meeting with this most prominent and respected Nevadan to ask if we could honor him at a fundraising gala. This gala could potentially net $25,000, a huge sum at the time.

I anguished over the meeting. One could only get an audience with a man of his stature once in a lifetime so I mustn't mess it up. I was frantic getting ready for the appointment, practicing the opening lines over and over. I needed an ice breaker: "Nice office," or "Nice tie," or "Boy, it sure is hot today," or "Is that your family in the photo?"

I fretted over what to wear. Would a business suit or mom-on-a-mission casual inspire more confidence?

What if I tripped and fell on my face? I had done that once before upon arriving at a charity "awareness event" at the showpiece home of a local socialite. As I stepped into the foyer, one high heel decided to part ways with its shoe, sending me flying across the entry hall and slamming me into a grand piano while the pianist continued, apprising me coolly.

I met a lifelong friend and future board member at that event when he kindly rushed over to pick me up and dust me off. He was a prominent architect, and he and his wife remarked that I had stolen the show with my grand entrance. I loved them for that face-saving remark. I still do, thirty-five years later.

I knew I must not go to that meeting with E. Parry Thomas filled with self-defeating thoughts.

Stay positive, Smith. Keep your eye on the finish line.

Riding up in the elevator, my confidence waned. The higher the floors, the more nervous I became. I was about to ask the most revered man in Nevada to give up his time, his valuable name and his privacy, and agree to help me raise thousands of dollars for a charity that he likely had very little interest in.

What if he said no right away; what would I do? And more importantly, what would I say to Governor O'Callaghan when I called to tell him I failed?

The elevator doors opened into a grand reception area on the top floor of the Valley Bank, and I took in the lavish surroundings. After a brief introduction, Mr. Thomas' impeccably clad assistant ushered me into his luxurious office that featured expensive art work on the walls and family photos on the credenza.

I was offered a seat across from him, and I noticed that his huge, impressive desk was completely devoid of papers, pens, and the usual accoutrements of business. It was the largest desk I had ever seen, and it spoke volumes about this man's personality.

Mr. Thomas was no nonsense, down to business, respectful, efficient, and welcoming as he stood and shook my hand.

A business meeting was like a carefully orchestrated dance, and the tone was typically set at hello. This was a very important meeting, and it was clear that I needed to respect this man's time. Perhaps I should have asked how much of it I had been allotted so I wouldn't overstay my welcome.

Or perhaps after quick introductions were made, I could have said, "Thank you for agreeing to meet with me, Mr. Thomas. Governor O'Callaghan said to say hello and also thank you. I want to respect your valuable time and get right to the point of my visit."

That's what I should have said.

Instead, all the rehearsing went out the window. I did away with the small talk and inane pleasantries and got right to the point of my visit, launching into a ten-minute diatribe without ever taking a breath. I was so nervous that my mouth got intensely dry as I jabbered away. I was a rank amateur out of my league.

I babbled on explaining the event and why we wanted to honor him, telling him about the charity: its inception, its history, why we needed to raise $25,000 to retrofit our derelict building, how his attendance at the event would insure attendance, and why Governor Mike and I thought it would be simply fabulous if he would agree.

In the middle of my sermon, I noticed his eyes flickering toward the open door, so I took a deep breath and continued. He was looking at me with amazement, measuring my never-ending stream of words as he waited to get a word in.

In time, his eyes went to his watch, and I began to perspire. I was blowing it. I was also afraid if I stopped talking he would have me thrown out. Launching into my best material, I took another stab saying I had a son who would one day be old enough to be served by this charity. After another tirade, I stopped for a heartbeat to take another gulp of air, and he found the opportunity to interject.

"I will give you $25,000 if you don't honor me."

This stopped me dead in my tracks.

I sat speechless as he quickly strode over and helped me to my feet. After shaking my hand and telling me that he was happy to help, he passed me off to his assistant and closed the door, instructing her to write a check right away.

I had just raised $25,000 in ten minutes and was both elated and mortified. This was not the outcome I had envisioned.

As I rode down in the elevator with the check clutched in my hand, my face burned crimson red from the embarrassment of what had just taken place.

I had failed. I hadn't shown any interest in what made him tick or what his interests were, a cardinal sin in building relationships. I broke all the rules of a professional fundraiser, including eyes and ears before mouth.

Poor Mr. Thomas didn't have a chance to tell me about himself, about his amazing life and family. As soon as I found a public phone, I dialed the number and made the dreaded call to Governor O'Callaghan.

Instead of telling me what a moron I was, Governor Mike laughed heartily and was very pleased. "Smith, let's find ten more people who don't want to be honored and send you on your way."

And so he did. I met face-to-face with nine more powerful men in the gaming and hotel industry and other businesses. Each time I came away with a check for $25,000, which combined with all the others would be worth over a million dollars today. I told them I was on a roll, and in Las Vegas, you don't mess with that kind of luck.

But not all donations came so easily. I had my share of bad luck, too.

My early foray into major gift fundraising put me in front of one of Las Vegas' most venerated families. There was one notable family who made their fortune in the construction business, and when fundraisers discussed the ten most-respected families in Las Vegas, they were at the top of the list.

The call came in from the son of the patriarch himself, two days before Christmas in 1980.

"I have a gift from our family foundation and would like you to come over and pick it up now."

Unsolicited donations were rare, and as such, I was not going to let the grass grow under my feet. I jumped into my car on a mission to retrieve the check.

The office was in an old building downtown. He motioned for me to take a seat on the couch in his dimly-lit office, and then he sat down uncomfortably close right next to me,

Light banter ensued as we surveyed each other. I was anxious to get the donation in my hand and leave. Sensing the intimate mood in the room and a potential proposition coming my way, I stood and announced that I had to be back for an office party in a few minutes.

With that the donor also stood and offered me a check for $5,000, which was a huge sum at the time, and said, "This is a donation from our company. We had a successful year and admire the work that you do, and our family wanted to give you this check. The only condition is that it not go to the retards."

Shocked by his declaration, I stammered, asking what he meant.

His face was awash with gyrations and facial contortions as he said, "You know, I don't want the money to go the retards. You know, the ones whose mothers do drugs and then crank out retards. The lazy ones, you know, the retards."

I put my hand out, grabbed the check, and fled. I am not proud that I took the check, but that family continued to contribute over the years. Dirty money that I made sure went directly to the "retards."

CHAPTER THIRTY-NINE

PEOPLE

"Was there a Chinaman in the woodshed?"

Shortly after Chris was born, I met a woman who was an ardent fan of Glenn's. We were appearing at the Bonaventure Hotel in Montreal, and like so many fans who found ways to access celebrities, she wheedled her way backstage after the show.

Upon encountering me and our newborn child, she cooed solicitously until unspoken words formed on her lips as she attempted to reconcile his features. She couldn't quite put her finger on it, but she knew my boy was unique. He was exceptionally beautiful, and in the Downs lottery of life, he had lucked out, escaping the flat, simian features, the small, abnormally-shaped ears and thickened, protruding tongue.

Finally, the woman inquired about his upturned eyes.

"Was there a Chinaman in the woodshed?" she asked, laughing at her own cleverness.

Glancing at Glenn, I replied as kindly as possible, "Not that I know of. . .but our son Christopher does have Down syndrome. This is a condition that causes him to have devel-opmental delays."

Her eyes grew bigger and her mouth opened and closed with the demeanor of a child caught in the act of stealing a cookie. Eventually she recovered. Then she held both hands in the air, each a foot away from her head, and said,

"Oooh. . .thank God he is not one of those, ahhh, you know, Mongoloid idiots. You know the ones with the big heads."

When Chris was still an infant, I read an article by noted sociologist Simon Olshansky, director of the Special Children's Clinic in Cambridge, Massachusetts, who wrote, "Most parents who have a mentally defective child suffer chronic sorrow throughout their lives, regardless of whether the child is kept at home or put away. These parents have very little to look forward to; they will always be burdened by the child's unrelenting needs, demands, and unabated dependency. The woes, the trials, the moments of despair will continue until either their own deaths or the child's death. Release from the chronic sorrow may be obtainable only through death."

Geez. . .let's march this kid straight to Auschwitz.

Now I am drawn to people who are struggling. I was at the Toronto Post Office with Chris on a cold day in December. An early snow had blanketed the city, followed by an icy rain, catching everyone unprepared. There were long lines of impatient customers on a mission to get their parcels delivered in time for the holidays.

The tension in the post office was beginning to show on my little toddler's face. He was on the verge of tears. His extra chromosome made him extra sensitive, and he could pick up on different moods in a flash, be it sadness, danger, discomfort, happiness, or joy. Like a human barometer, he could gauge human emotion. My kid was a spiritual genius.

I was number five in line when an elderly woman in an oversize coat with a babushka on her head, shuffled up to the counter. With a wavering smile on her face, she tried to explain in broken English to a disinterested post office employee that she wanted her package to go to El Salvador, and she needed to know if she had enough stamps on the brown-paper-wrapped box, which was loosely tied with string.

The impatient clerk pulled at the string and berated the woman for her sloppy, substandard wrapping. Exasperated, he told everyone within earshot that he couldn't understand a word she was saying.

The woman struggled on in fractured sentences, eventually wilting from the look of disgust on his face and from the public humiliation he'd just laid upon her.

Chris' distress was palpable as he stiffened his little body and flailed his arms and legs and cast about in his stroller while people looked impassively on. He began to whimper, and I began to seethe.

She asked her question again, but the clerk was having none of it. With a conspiratorial nod and a wink to the rest of us designated accomplices, the government worker flippantly dismissed the woman telling her, *"No comprende. NEXT!"*

People looked on, nonplussed. Chris squirmed in his stroller wearing his angst like a crucifix tattooed on his forehead. Without resolving the issue, the clerk dismissed her once more, shouting, "Next."

The poor woman shuffled to the side, tears promising to erupt. I was boiling, outraged for this poor soul who, like all of us, invested considerable time in line on a simple mission to send a package home. Looking around, expecting to see the outrage on the faces of others, I saw that no one cared.

"Excuse me. I clearly heard this lady ask you if she needed extra stamps on her package. *What* part of her question could you not understand?"

With that, I grabbed the package from the lady, and slammed it on the counter. *"Tell* her what she needs for her package."

It's interesting to witness the change in attitude when indignation raises its ugly head. It can quickly make way for compromise. The postal worker at the counter was no longer smirking, as he looked about for help from others, who looked like they were having their own miserable day.

"Lady, I can't understand her," the clerk retorted.

"Well I clearly understood her and so did everyone else," I said.

With that I turned to the others in line, expecting them to back me up. "We all understood her question, right?"

Sadly, each person in line averted their eyes, scanning the ceiling, nervously checking their watch, the floor, or the person in line next to them. No one wanted any part of this scene.

What kind of a world do we live in when such cruelty and insensitivity can be inflicted on another human being?

Exasperated, I yelled, "Weigh it, for Christ's sake! And tell her if she has the required number of stamps!" The clerk said, in a more subdued tone, "What about the string? It's loose."

I pushed the gift in front of him and said, "THEN FIX IT. CHRISTMAS WILL BE OVER BY THE TIME YOU FINISH WITH THIS ONE CUSTOMER."

Chris was now smiling.

I tell this story not to demonstrate my own intolerance for intolerance, but to showcase the teachings from my son and to point out an intellectual awareness in my "throw-away child." With Chris as my teacher, I have come to learn that when we allow ourselves to appreciate and welcome vulnerable people, we discover just how flawed we are—how much we lack the qualities of the heart that they so inherently possess.

Chris had strengthened me, opened my mind to the possibilities. He had made me a warrior mom and a woman who also saw the world through rose-colored lenses. I was an optimist on steroids who believed "no" just got me closer to a "yes."

His birth introduced me to diverse, caring, generous, intelligent people from far-flung places. He opened my eyes to the need for awareness, support, and tolerance in order to advance the cause. Through him I met the loveliest people, embraced the naysayers, and removed all detractors from our lives.

My unique child attracted all types: people who donated their resources for the good of mankind; major philanthropists who gave breathtaking gifts; and successful business leaders and wonderful human beings who shared their largess and their hearts.

Through Christopher, I met celebrities who supported my efforts, who lent their bigger-than-life names to advance and dispel myths and misconceptions about the disabled.

People like Celine Dion, Robin Leach, Gilda Radner, Penn and Teller, Don Rickles, and more—all personal friends and amazingly kind people who might not be in my life without this extraordinary child.

And then there was Wayne Newton, a Las Vegas icon and legend, a mega-superstar and lifelong friend. As his star shone ever brighter, he championed disability and raised millions of dollars fighting alongside our family in our quest to bring awareness to the plight of the disabled, and, more personally, to bring Christopher into the country. Wayne's kind heart and sweet support of everything we struggled through brought legions of followers to our doorstep.

After the successful Aladdin afternoon concert, I got home and found Glenn with Eunice Kennedy Shriver Pat Kennedy Lawford, Ruth Carter Stapleton, and my star-struck mother, who was taking care of Chris. The women had been invited to the Newton home, and Glenn, who befriended Eunice Shriver and the Kennedy clan at the concert, was their escort.

Glenn had suggested stopping by our house first, which was just a few blocks from Wayne's Casa de Shenandoah estate so they could meet Christopher, who was a Special Olympics athlete. We also happened to be a poster family for the International Special Olympics.

There was no time to call everyone I knew and tell them that three sisters of American presidents were in my kitchen with Chris, who was eating yogurt and smiling while Eunice asked him questions about his various sports. Chris was dazzled by the attention and fascinated by the Kennedy accents.

As Eunice went on about his swimming medals, he held his spoon midair, waiting for her to finish so he could stuff his little mouth, but she must have gone on too long because after a while, Chris said, "Aww SHIT" and flipped his spoonful of yogurt at the illustrious trio.

To diffuse the embarrassment, it was suggested the ladies might want to go outside and watch Chris swim; after all, he was a Special Olympian Gold medalist!

That sounded like a good plan, so they took off their shoes and stockings, hiked their skirts up, and sat on the pool deck with their feet in the water while they watched Chris. What a fabulously comfortable group of women they were.

It was not lost on me that these were very famous and accomplished women. Eunice Shriver was the founder of Special Olympics and National Institute of Child Health and Human Development, and an Awardee of the Medal of Freedom, She was recognized worldwide for her work on behalf of those with intellectual disabilities, and was the sister of John F. Kennedy, the most venerated president of our times.

Eunice's sister, Pat Lawford Kennedy had married Hollywood heartthrob Peter Lawford, who introduced their brother, John F. Kennedy to Marilyn Monroe.

And to round things out, Ruth Carter Stapleton was the evangelist sister of President Jimmy Carter.

I was so proud that my son was entertaining the sisters of presidents—that is until he surfaced with a burst and gave them a really good soaking. When I thought about this little boy whose future looked so bleak, I couldn't help but smile at all the special and magical moments.

Through Christopher, I met casino mogul Ralph Engelstad, a kind and generous man, who came into my life during my first few years in Las Vegas. When Chris was five years old, I volunteered with Special Olympics. Hockey stars Bobby Hull and Gordy Howe of the Toronto Maple Leafs were coming to Vegas, and I was enlisted to help them put together a Special Olympics Golf Tournament.

I had to line up some donors, and this brought me to the doorstep of Ralph Engelstad, a self-made multi-millionaire who earned his first million by age thirty. He was the sole owner of the Imperial Palace in Biloxi and Las Vegas. Ralph, an avowed fan of all things hockey, was a natural candidate to join the cause.

To say I was nervous to meet this man was an understatement. Mr. Engelstad was a Las Vegas legend, who had many detractors due to his business acumen and controversial nature. He had a reputation as a hard-nosed negotiator, a tough guy who had scrabbled his way to the top. He was one of the most successful and respected casino operators in town and through a favor from a friend, I was now meeting him.

With Christopher in tow, I made my way to his office. As I entered the elevator on the ground floor, I was followed by a man in blue jeans and a shirt with an IP logo, who was carrying a broom. I asked him for directions, and he offered to accompany me to the executive offices.

On the elevator, this kind man with sparkling eyes showered affection on Christopher and made funny faces with him as we rode to the top floor. I tried to quell the butterflies forming as I anticipated my meeting with the business scion and legendary industry tycoon. The closer I got to the office, the more anxious I became, wondering if he would be annoyed that I brought my child to a meeting and send me packing.

When we got to the top floor, the janitor pointed in the direction of the office and bowed with a flourish like a troubadour with a cape. Chris thought this was very funny and said, "Aww Shit," the two words he knew the best. The man laughed, and with a twinkle in his eyes, walked toward the door, stepped inside, and introduced himself as Ralph Engelstad.

I was enchanted by this man whose reputation as a gruff casino operator belied the truth of his generosity and charm. I later learned he had a hiring policy that included the employment of a commensurate percentage of disabled-to-non-disabled staff, going against the tradition of the day when excluding disabled workers from mainstream society was the popular practice.

The result of the meeting was a "yes" to my request and a lifetime friendship. Little did either of us know that he would become one of the most influential figures in my life and in the lives of so many families like mine.

Ralph Engelstad and his family were some of the most significant agents of social change in the country for the disabled, and through their visionary leadership gifts, they changed peoples' perceptions about the value of kids like Christopher.

And they did it without any fanfare. It was only after Ralph Engelstad passed away that the community became aware of his kindness and largess as one of the foremost supporters of disability in Nevada and the country,

Like so many others, I admired this man and his family deeply. A testament to their inherent charitable ways was the day they presented me with a check for $35 million, the largest gift ever donated to the world of disability.

I had come a long way from homelessness to disability-advocate Mom to asking for a historic gift. How could I not succeed with friends like these?

CHAPTER FORTY

SIBLINGS

*I quickly realized that having a "normal" child
was no cake walk either.*

Seven years after Christopher's entry into the world, his
brother, Jason, was born. Jason was a beautiful, robust,
healthy baby, who weighed ten pounds and entered the world
squalling, looking like he was ready to stand up and walk on
his own two feet right out of the hospital.

Jason's circumstances were as dissimilar to Chris' as identical twins are similar. It was a calm pregnancy spent with
my feet up reading lots of books. There were early warning
signs of the impending arrival and a stroll to the hospital. It
seemed that Jason's birth was attended by half of Las Vegas.
Friends of every ilk crowded into the waiting room and lobby:
celebrities, bartenders, cocktail waiters, blackjack dealers,
charity board members and more.

There were no bets being waged on an airplane about the weight, sex, or birthdate of this already beloved boy and his relieved mother.

When Chris was born, I lost all the weight I had gained in one day, leaving the hospital looking like I had never given birth. With Jason's arrival, it was several months before people stopped asking me when my baby was due. I was fat and happy and so was my new baby. Flowers filled the hospital room and the biggest, most beautiful display imaginable was from Wayne Newton, who had signed on to be Jason's godfather. His godmother would be my longtime friend Debbie Jackson.

Jason's christening was a show business occasion with a cornucopia of Strip entertainers, members of the mafia, Sands impresario Walter Kane, and many hotel executives and political figures in attendance. The cake was created by Chef Ty (Caesars Palace's head bakery chef) and emblazoned with the words "Congratulations on Your Concert of Love!"

After we brought Jason home, Christopher never left his side, peering at him in his bassinet for hours, seemingly in awe of this new arrival into our home and family. In time, Christopher taught Jason by example how not to drown in the pool. At eighteen months, Jason could paddle end, tread water, and occasionally dive down in the deep end of the pool for a toy. He was an amazing child, and, like his dad, a musical prodigy, playing piano by age three.

With Jason, I quickly realized that having a "normal" child was no cake walk. He got into as much mischief as he could, running full speed into every room, getting into every nook and cranny in the house. When speaking or presenting to large groups of people, I often posed the question, "Who in the room has a normal, healthy child?" When hands were held high, I would respond, "My heart goes out to you. No doctor prepared me for my healthy child."

Many siblings of a disabled family member grow up resenting that family member, often embarrassed by their peculiar brother or sister. I have known people who it has taken many, many years to finally admit they had a disabled sibling or child. I am always surprised why they cast them out of their life, but then who am I to judge. When given Christopher's diagnosis, I wanted him to die.

Having a family member with a profound disability was daunting, not for the faint of heart. Many siblings erase this "flawed" relative from their life, even from their memory. Although born to the same mother and father that sibling would never be their peer or a co-conspirator in the face of parental injustice. The truth was that no child growing up with a special needs family member would have a normal life, but maybe therein lies the beauty. After all, who wants to be ordinary?

The "normal" sibling almost always lived in second place, while the "broken" child always took center stage. For a parent, all available energy and resources were spent on the needs of the disabled child, while the remaining family members took a back seat.

And yet such high expectations were placed on the "normal" child. *This child was born disabled, but here is our beautiful, more accomplished "other" child!*

I recall a kindergarten teacher telling us that Jason might have Attention Deficit Disorder. He would arrive at school singing songs and daydreaming, appearing to be in a faraway land. I was furious hearing this quick diagnosis of my "normal" child. No. Christopher was my damaged child... not Jason!

What the hell was she talking about? This "undamaged son" could play piano and even compose songs like Mozart did, for goodness sake! He was a musical genius. My "normal" child was thoughtful, introspective, and kind. Look at his picture. . .see? He tied balloons to the dead garden lizard and sent him to heaven.

Chris loved his little brother, who quickly surpassed him in every way and became his hero and protector. Growing up with a Down syndrome sibling was a lesson in patience, sensitivity, and consideration. Day after day, Jason could be seen with his arms around his big brother, loving him intensely. As Jason got older, he learned compassion and a perspective that can only be gleaned firsthand from recognizing the reality of Christopher's place in the world. He taught his friends that same love. If you didn't accept Chris, you would not be Jason's friend. Those were Jason's rules.

I remember a day I misjudged his intentions. It was Jason's first day in high school, and like most kids, he was anxious. I drove him to school, and as we got closer, he made me pull over well in advance, out of sight of the hundreds of kids who were assembling in front of the school. He didn't want his friends to see he needed a ride from his mom.

As he tentatively ambled on his way, I sat in my car in a defensive mode. If any of these high school kids took issue with my kid, I would be one crazy mother. Jason was eventually greeted by some of his friends. They too were nervous about their first day in a new school, but I could see him visibly relax when he spotted his buddies.

I was relieved too, and was ready to make a U-turn and drive off when I noticed the entire school assembly was staring intently with mouths open at something across the street.

What was going on?

Hundreds of kids in large and small groups were watching, laughing pointing, or whispering. Then I saw the object of the stares. A young man, a little person with his backpack weighing him down, was determinedly walking toward the school.

I turned to look at Jason. He and his friends were nervously talking and looking at the little person, too. My heart broke for this young man with dwarfism, and I was becoming very angry with these insensitive kids, including my own.

And then Jason magically broke away from his friends and walked up to the young man, engaged him in conversation, and they walked together to the school.

My heart swelled, and tears formed. This was the essence of who this boy had become. We were all better people for having a family member who didn't fit into society's norms. What lessons in kindness had we learned? Growing up with a disabled child gave us all a truly unique perspective. I had the deepest respect and appreciation for what Jason endured as Chris' brother and for the love that he displayed.

Throughout his school years, Jason would gather the school rejects to his side. He would befriend the friendless and welcome them into his inner circle. I was proud and grateful for this son who always took a back seat to his brother.

And yes, it turned out that he did have Attention Deficit Disorder.

CHAPTER \ FORTY-ONE

CHRISTOPHER THE HERO

No one wanted their child to get too close to this strange kid who could stay underwater longer than Jacques Cousteau.

At the bottom of our swimming pool was an image of a dolphin. It was placed on the pool's plaster surface at the midway point from the steps as a whimsical feature for the kids to delight in. Chris loved this dolphin and would jabber away to it from the steps, while kicking his legs in the water.

There have been many studies about the interaction of humans and dolphins and the dolphins' sensitivity to people with special needs. Most theories have been debunked, but nonetheless, I can unequivocally say that my boy communed with this tile dolphin more than with any of us. In the winter, he would stand outside by the water's edge, rocking back and forth in a conversation known only to him. When the weather warmed, he would swim down to his inlaid dolphin friend and hang out at the bottom of the pool, blowing bubbles in "underwater speak," improbably lying down next to his tile buddy, turning on his back to look up at us from under the water. My kid was amazing and could hold his breath forever, much longer than seemed humanly possible.

On a sizzling hot summer day when Christopher was eight years old, the family gathered with friends at a local public swimming pool. Chris, being an accomplished swimmer, jumped with abandon into the water and splashed with glee. I sat with friends on the side of the pool with Jason, who delighted in watching his big brother's antics and unadulterated joy as Chris goofily showed off, doing handstands and swimming circles around every other child that day.

The pool, which was one of the only public swimming facilities in Vegas at the time, was filled to capacity with families enjoying a quick dip and the occasional headlong dive. That day my small family was an object of curiosity. Glenn, with his entertainer's good looks, gold chain, and medallion emblazoned with his kids' names on both sides, strummed his guitar, while I, a young mom with long blond pigtails and a chubby baby, had a "special child" in tow.

I have found on occasion that some people kindly showed interest and treated me just like any other mom. They might make small talk, or nervously eyeball Chris, or make tentative inquiries, while others simply looked straight through us as though we didn't exist, or—I love this one—state that they have a "retarded cousin" and they "understood what I was dealing with."

Not so on this day.

My boy was jumping in the deep end with his odd swimming style and underwater stunts when I noticed parents beginning to put their arms protectively around their kids.

I soon realized Chris was not just an object of curiosity, he scared them. No one wanted their child to get too close to this strange kid who could stay underwater longer than Jacques Cousteau. Chris soon had the pool to himself.

As I took this all in, the idyllic family outing suddenly turned disastrous. Screams pierced the air as people yelled that a child was drowning. Shocked parents dashed along the edge of the pool to make sure it wasn't their own child and then pointed and dove in.

Terrified like everyone else, I took note of Chris in the pool and then Jason who was right there in my arms. Then I saw the toddler, submerged in the deep end. I wondered how long this baby had been underwater. At that moment, to my horror and everyone else's, my Chris could be seen advancing like a torpedo from the deepest depths of the water. Homing in on the drowning child, he scooped him up.

In slow motion, I watched this cataclysmic scene play out, envisioning the horror on peoples' faces when they read tomorrow's newspaper headline.

Toddler drowns in pool while unattended disabled child and his terrible neglectful mother finish him off.

I saw myself being led away in handcuffs, with people condemning me to hell for not paying closer attention to this kid who shouldn't be in *their* pool in the first place. It's amazing how all those visions had time to play out in a few split seconds.

There was my kid, whom the crowd perceived as a "retard," about to kill a baby. And then, like he was shot out of a cannon, he soared up out of the water, baby in tow. He easily lifted his treasure onto the side of the pool as shocked people rushed over.

What did my son do next? He simply brushed his hands off and went right back to swimming.

Pandemonium set in. The people in the water were now scrambling to get out and help resuscitate the child. As this drama unfolded, my Chris was joyfully swimming. He now had the entire pool to himself and he was one happy boy.

He would never know that he saved a baby's life that day. He instinctively did the right thing, knowing the baby was in trouble. The baby survived, and my amazing boy was a hero. Love personified, my son's sweetness and innocence saved the day. He was Superman, and yet no one thanked him. He was an angel unaware, who taught me lessons every day. He worked hard to make me a better mom, forcing me to see my own shortcomings and failings. It was and continues to be a difficult journey.

When Chris was ten years old, (a hallmark year since Chris' early prognosis was that he would be dead by that age), I was cleaning the house when I happened upon him staring at his reflection in the mirror. He held a toothbrush that I had just given him ten minutes earlier, in midair, nowhere near his teeth, as he studied his own image staring back at him. Engrossed, he turned to one side and then to the other to get a better view. He was mesmerized by his reflection.

I often wondered if Chris knew he was different from other kids. Low-functioning, developmentally disabled people didn't realize how restricted their lives were. They weren't capable of fully recognizing or understanding life with all its many colors.

Because Chris was nonverbal, we had never had a chance to pose such questions to him. Chris was multiply disabled, suffering a myriad of related issues including mental health, autism, and chronic obsessive-compulsive behaviors. People with Down syndrome have smaller brains and are at increased risk for depression, psychosis, disruptive-behavior disorders, and anxiety.

Why is he staring at his reflection so intently? Is he just now realizing he is different?

I passed by the bathroom once more, peering through the crack in the door to see if he would indeed brush his teeth or wait for me to come in and do the job for him. He couldn't see me, and I decided I would wait it out. *Let's see who is the most stubborn, buddy.* I hunkered down, peering at him from my secret spot.

Watching him scrutinize his features from all angles eventually caused a lump to form in my throat. I could clearly see that he was taking in the full measure of himself.

Was he taking note of his short stature, his little features, his ears that were just a bit lower than they should be, and his upward slanting eyes?

He turned this way and that, looking at himself at every angle.

Oh boy, now what? Is he seeing how different he is from the mainstream homo sapiens world? Would this create even more problems? Would he be bitter? Angry? Sad?

All these thoughts were going through my head as I watched my little guy circumspectly appraise his image. I teared up. This was the day that I never wanted to witness, a day when my boy would look accusatorially at me and say in so many unspoken words, *"You did this to me. . .You caused this."*

Oh, the heartache I felt. *How could I protect him? How could I take away the hurt and guard him from the cruelty and pain he would surely endure?*

And then my boy saved the day once more, giving his mirror image a broad smile, a wink, and a thumbs-up.

"I am one cool guy," he was surely thinking. I dissolved into a puddle of tears.

He had accepted his lot in life, so why couldn't I? If I had not had the opportunity to be his mom, I would have missed the most enriching, rewarding experiences in life. He gave me hope and the strength to be a good mom.

Because of him, I found myself on an exciting journey to uncover all his miraculous attributes, and in doing so, I uncovered his secret to grace and beauty. He possessed an inexplicable intelligence that caused me to see my faults and allowed me to speak softly and gently to my heart in a way that revealed my soul. Christopher was providing me with daily lessons in compassion and empathy. I was no longer the self-absorbed entertainer I once was; my life had new meaning. I had learned empathy and generosity and was a reflection of my son's light.

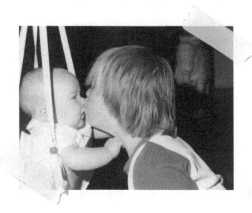 

CHAPTER FORTY-TWO

THE SOCK AND THE THIEF

*When Chris was seven years old and Jason newly home
from his arrival into our lives, a thief came into our home.*

It was nine-o-clock on a Friday evening. My mother, who by
now was living with us in Las Vegas full time, was sleeping
in her upstairs bedroom, while Chris slept alongside her in a
makeshift bed. He had given up his own room in deference
to his aunts, uncles, and cousins, who had come for a visit.

Glenn and his family were playing a game of pool, while I
stacked raffle tickets in batches of one hundred at the kitchen
table. The tickets were to be distributed to willing volunteers
to sell for the upcoming Concert of Love.

Inexplicably, a sudden cool breeze shifted the drapes and
scattered my small piles.

Who let the dog out? I thought.

A movement on the periphery of my vision silently called out, and I looked up, startled to see a ghostly apparition that turned out to be my mother. My eyes widened at the sight of her—white face, hair in disarray, a rumpled nightgown swaying around her legs—she pointed across the upstairs landing.

"Rob-ber."

She didn't speak nor whisper the word. She simply mouthed it. Then she cupped her mouth, imploring a silent urgent scream to come forth to no avail. Her mouth formed the soundless words. "Ro. . .ro. . .ROBBER!"

I stared at her confused, the clacking of the pool balls and the laughter in the other room were the only sounds in the house. Another breeze scattered more tickets and the curtains in a discordant dance.

What on earth was she saying?

Her mouth contorted, pleading, my mother mouthed the words once more. "ROBBER."

I gawked up at her. "Mom, are you okay?"

She pointed to the end of the hall once more, and put a finger to her lips shushing me.

I wondered if she was sleepwalking.

"ROBBER," she finally said.

A slow realization hit me. *Is she saying robber? In our home? Now?*

"Mom, what? There's a thief in the house?"

Finally liberated by my openly-stated question, she screamed a piercing declaration, "ROBBER! HELP! HELP! THERE IS A ROBBER IN THE HOUSE!" and promptly plopped to the floor.

Pandemonium broke out, and adrenalin kicked in as the men took the stairs two at a time, pool cues in hand, while I ran in circles looking for some kind of weapon to defend my home.

It seemed a thief had climbed the circular wrought iron steps in the backyard to the roof and entered my mother's unlocked bedroom from the upstairs landing. Once inside, he encountered her in bed with Christopher sound asleep next to her.

Holding a pillow in his hand, as though to stifle someone's screams or smother someone to death, he cautioned her to stay calm.

"Where is your purse?"

She motioned to an overstuffed purse on the counter; no, she had no jewelry; everything she had was in that purse and he could have it.

Purse in hand, he warned her to stay quiet, and silently crept out of her room. While I was obliviously counting tickets downstairs, he entered another bedroom undetected, where he found my father-in-law's bulging wallet. Then he crossed the hall to my small office. Finding nothing of value there, he exited soundlessly through the French doors and across the rooftop parapet.

After the police left, we talked throughout the night. It was frightening to think that a thief would be so bold as to enter a home full of adults who were awake. And how brave was my mother, whose instinct was to protect Chris by remaining calm and not unnerving the burglar.

We discussed the events ad nauseam. The police said the pillow could have been used as a silencer for a gun. They said a man with a gun had recently invaded a home nearby with tragic consequences. They said we were lucky, that it could have been worse.

There were moments of humor, too. It turned out my mother's purse was packed with raffle tickets to sell and my father-in-law's wallet was bereft of cash, but full of clipped coupons for free slot play and two-for-one buffets, which were found strew across the neighborhood the next morning.

Everyone needed a break the next day, so Glenn hitched up the boat and took his visiting family members to Lake

Mead. Mom and I were still shaken by what had transpired and exhausted from the lack of sleep, so we opted to stay home with the kids and get some rest.

We sat in the living room discussing what might have been happened had my mother's cool head not prevailed, while Chris, who seemed unperturbed by the drama and the presence of the police the night before, sat outside in his favorite chair by the pool, happily twirling his sock, his blue eyes mesmerized by its repetitive movement, musing in a language known only to him.

The cops and forensic technicians had spent considerable time in the upstairs bedrooms, and Chris had been entertained as they fingerprinted the doorknobs and took the imprints of the intruder's feet on the outdoor staircase.

Chris easily picks up on moods and danger, but he was off in his own world, none the worse for wear. Oh, what I wouldn't have given to climb inside that little Down syndrome head and view the world from his extra chromosome perspective, from the secret world he inhabits.

For a period of time, peace reigned. Mom and I had nothing more to say as Jason took a nap next to us.

Then we heard a noise on the roof.

CLOMP, CLOMP, CLOMP! What was that? CLOMP, CLOMP, CLOMP...Oh, good GOD, the thief was back!

"Run!"

Jumping up, I grabbed Jason, and propelled my shocked mother out the front door, fleeing the house and the monster on the roof.

Out on the street, we were confronted with chaos. Cop cars could be heard approaching, their sirens blaring, while concerned neighbors gathered outside. Across the street, a man with flailing arms excitedly jumped up and down, directing the cop cars to my house where they screeched to a full stop.

"There he is, up there, on the roof!" shouted the neighbor.

Police hopped out of their cars and hurriedly cordoned off the area, ushering the spectators and my family out of harm's way.

"Whose house is this?" they asked.

"It's mine," I managed to say. "We were robbed last night. We heard footsteps just now. . . they must have come back."

"Could you tell how many people were on your roof?"

"Not really. One or two, I think."

"Is there anyone else in the home?"

"No, just me, my baby Jason, and my mother. We heard footsteps on the roof and we ran as soon as we. . ." and then a gradual realization, "Oh no! My son Christopher is in the back yard in his lounge chair. He's eight and disabled!"

I couldn't believe I had left him behind.

More cops arrived and blocked the street while others piled out of their cars with their guns drawn, taking aim at my roof. I tried to imagine my defenseless Chris all by himself in the backyard while his mother fled to safety.

A megaphone appeared, as an officer called out to the intruder "Come out with your hands up. . .put your hands in the air where we can see you. . .come out with your hands up. . .RIGHT NOW!"

My neighbors and I stood in silence as the command was repeated several times. And then, just above the rooftop parapet, a slight movement, the tip of a white blurry object appeared, just a tiny inch at first, then a tad more as all of us spectators watched with bated breath. Then a small white sock took shape, followed by a pair of little slanted blue eyes. It was Christopher.

"STOP! IT'S MY SON!" I screamed, running toward the house, past the now shocked and bewildered officers.

What prompted our boy to take a stroll on the roof that day is a much talked about family mystery. Christopher, the kid who wouldn't step on a crack, had somehow managed to climb up the outdoor spiral staircase, over a two-foot parapet wall with a little sock in hand, to take a gander at the neighborhood and see what the fuss was all about.

Christopher knew more than he could ever tell us, but what he didn't know is that he became a legend that day with the story laughingly recounted in our home and precincts across the Las Vegas Valley.

CHAPTER FORTY-THREE

OVER A BARREL

"Yes. . .our son is illegal."

When Vice President Hubert Humphrey, our son's wonderful and generous sponsor died, there was still a one-year wait for Glenn and me to become American citizens.

His passing made it considerably harder for us to expedite our own citizenship. Harboring an illegal alien is a felony punishable by prison time and potential deportation. If we wanted to move forward with our own "naturalization" status, we would have to lie under oath because the first question asked on the citizenship application is, "Have you ever, or do you know of anyone who is, or has, harbored an illegal alien?"

What would we say? "Yes. . .us. . .our son is illegal."

The laws clearly state that it is a violation of law for any person to conceal, harbor, aid, or shield from detection in any place, any alien who is in the United States in violation of law.

Harboring, aiding, or abetting means any conduct that substantially enabled an alien to remain in the U.S. illegally. The sheltering need not be clandestine. This provision included harboring an alien who entered the U.S. legally, but has since lost his legal status. That was our boy!

It was also a felony to encourage or induce an alien to come to or reside in the U.S. knowingly or recklessly disregarding the fact that the alien's entry or residence was in violation of the law. Yup, that was us!

The penalty for felony harboring was a fine and up to ten years' imprisonment. Conspiracy to commit alien smuggling could carry the same penalties and thousands of dollars in fines.

At the time of the former vice president's death, Chris was eight years old. We never uttered a word about his illegal status to anyone other than our attorney for fear of being reported and removed from the country. And yet, while we were breaking immigration laws, we continued to raise funds and awareness for the disabled, and accepted every request for help.

Glenn traveled a lot, performing across the United States in New York, Oklahoma, California, and Nevada, as well as outside the country in Canada and South America. We worked hard, paid our taxes, and were good citizens. It was just this little alien kid who had us over a barrel.

We also knew that if Chris didn't become a legal U.S. citizen before the age of eighteen, he would no longer be eligible to enter the country on his parents' merits. At age eighteen, he would be considered an adult and would be required to take English and civics tests. He would be required to recite the Pledge of allegiance and have to have basic knowledge of United States history and government.

There was no way Chris could pass those tests or any tests, other than one for being the cutest Down syndrome child ever. He could drive a go-cart in circles, sing along to Elton John's "Goodbye Yellow Brick Road," and swim like a fish, but recite the Pledge of Allegiance? It was impossible. There was absolutely no hope of Chris gaining legal status after he turned eighteen.

We continued to try and make lemonade out of an impossible situation. Behind the scenes, friends from Arc, their Government Relations Director, Paul Marchand, and U.S. Arc board member Elizabeth Boggs, toiled away for years on our behalf.

Chris could no longer travel to Canada to see his grandparents and many adoring cousins, aunts, and uncles. For years, whenever Glenn had an appearance in Canada, I would stay behind in Las Vegas, or we would call upon relatives to travel to Vegas and watch Chris while we were away. When Chris was eight, my mother came to stay with us for the summer and never left.

Chris thrived in Las Vegas. He attended segregated schools for the disabled. He was at Variety for his first year, and then Helen J. Stewart for the remainder of his education. He participated in Special Olympics, winning medals in swimming and track. His medals were not for crossing the finish line, however, because he never grasped the concept of competition. No matter how hard we cheered him on, he had another plan for winning.

In a swim heat or track event, he could be seen easily leading the pack, long strokes when swimming, a loping, joyous jog when running as legs took off in disparate directions somehow propelling him forward. He would give us the "thumbs up" when he saw us on the sidelines and then inevitably he would stop midway to wait for another Olympian to catch up. To the endless frustration of his parents and little brother, Jason, Chris always crossed the finish line last.

In time, we began to see that his athletic prowess was not about his ability to cross the finish line first. It was instead a mission to participate in life on his own terms. He would be a champion for all seasons through his infinite capacity for love.

My Christopher, first out of the gate and last to cross the finish line, showed everyone what winning truly meant. He was born a true teacher to mankind. It's a privilege to be Christopher's mom; he is the most perfect, non-judgmental, and gentle person in the world, and in my view, it would be a better world if there were more people like my boy in it.

When Hubert Humphrey died, we lost more than a sponsor; we lost a disability champion and the dream of legalizing Chris. We were told by the attorneys we were completely out of options. Chris must leave the country and apply for re-entry from Canada.

We most certainly wouldn't do that. Las Vegas was our home. We were legal residents; we were simply not going to dump Chris on the other side of the border. Instead of panicking, we carried on, having faith that an answer would appear at some point before those ten years expired and Chris was banned forever from his adopted country.

CHAPTER FORTY-FOUR

TAKING ON THE GOVERNOR

"Go for their throats!"

As I fought for Chris' legalization in the U.S., I found myself fighting for all families of disabled children, and was often called upon to help small organizations across the country. Many disability groups like Opportunity Village began when a few families got together. Most were unsophisticated in their approach to philanthropy, and my conviction that raising funds meant they simply had to get out there and ask was a concept they had not considered. I enjoyed sharing the knowledge I had gained and raising the expectations of struggling organizations. If I couldn't save my son, I would save others.

As the senior fundraiser at Opportunity Village, I was given the chance to make a significant difference in the lives of so many people. I had been an actress, model, dancer, and mother to two wonderful children. Now I had the awesome responsibility of growing an organization and securing the funds for its future while making life better for some very special folks. It was a daunting job, and each day I questioned if I had what it took.

Upon joining the organization, there were many challenges to overcome. The original founders were revolutionaries and I was reverential of all they had accomplished to date, but they had lost interest in the day-to-day prospect of keeping the doors open. They were exhausted and rightfully so. The organization's Board of Directors was made up of well-meaning family members, most who were more focused on the personal development of their own children than the larger issues of a self-sustaining charity. These families had done something wonderful when they created this place out of sheer willpower and determination.

They had also created a monster that needed to be fed.

Funds to operate the organization had to be either earned or raised. My first few years were spent establishing fund-raising events like the Concert of Love, the Meatball Festival, and a seasonal gift-wrap booth at the Boulevard Mall.

In my first year, I completed a small capital campaign to provide a processing center to house donated goods for the thrift store. When it concluded on time and under budget, I was ready to take on a bigger challenge.

Thankfully, the seven founding families had the foresight to secure two and a half acres of land for future in an underdeveloped part of town, near Rainbow and Charleston Boulevard that would one day be considered in the heart of Las Vegas. The land was set aside in an agreement between Opportunity Village, the State of Nevada, the Bureau of Land Management (BLM), and the division of Mental Health and Mental Retardation. OV had a registered deed that had gone unnoticed for twenty-five years.

As an established fundraiser with several successful fundraising initiatives under my belt, it was an opportune time for me to plan for the next twenty-five years.

We would raise the money to build the very first campus designed for the use of our special population on six acres at a key Las Vegas intersection that would include an employment training center, life-skills and respite programs, social recreation and art programs, boardrooms, office suites, beautiful parklands and space for us to grow.

Given the competition for funding sources in a newly-conscious and developing city, the plan to launch a capital campaign was not without its detractors—ones in high places. By now I had pulled together a group of business leaders to take up the reins from the original founders. They in turn would bring in many community contacts to join the campaign. I enlisted the support of my mentor, former governor Mike O'Callaghan. Design meetings with board members and architects soon ensued, and renderings were made available for donors to review.

But as the fundraising commenced and the interest grew, a wrinkle appeared on the horizon. A big wrinkle. The State of Nevada got wind of our plans to build and promptly pulled the rug out from under us.

The chairman of the House Ways and Means Committee and the newly appointed governor contacted our board to tell them that the land was in fact not ours, but instead was government land set aside for education. According to them, the land we laid claim to was now projected to be built out for education facilities, and we were simply out of luck.

That was when I trudged off once more to the office of the "friend to the friendless," former governor Michael O'Callaghan. As I sat teary-eyed, relating details of the land-grab, he sputtered and fussed and finally yelled, "Oh, for God's sake Smith. . .QUIT YOUR SNIVELING. You are on the side of right and good. Why are you letting this happen? You go after them with a vengeance. Go for their throats!"

This was quite the endorsement, and *"Go for their throats"* I did. With calls to family members, donors, Rotary, Kiwanis, and Lions Club members, connected friends and local icons, a mighty army gathered.

It was clear we had friends in both high and low places. The media was on high alert, and a flurry of press releases and editorials were sent out daily. We organized a campaign comprised of hundreds of parents, and they and their friends called on legislators to demand the state give us the land that was rightfully ours.

Thousands of signatures from prominent community members were eventually gathered, spearheaded by Sahara Hotel magnate Paul Lowden. The state was bullying Opportunity Village, and it didn't sit well with many city leaders.

It was never clear to me why members of the state government would want to commit political suicide by taking our land away and taking on an organization that by now had become a beloved and respected charity.

In the end, we prevailed, and the land was deemed ours, but not before a press conference was called with the governor and senators in attendance. When asked why the change of heart, the governor's tongue-in-cheek reply was, "We were made to see the error of our ways."

CHAPTER FORTY-FIVE

THE FREEZER INCIDENT

Who would be inside a refrigerator and in need of a light?

My idea for a Magical Forest was born out of a deep desire to celebrate the season as well as the successful conclusion of a three year capital campaign that allowed us to build our first beautiful, one-of-a kind campus ahead of schedule and under budget. Our fundraising staff of three had defied the naysayers, raising $18 million in three short years.

The doubting politicos, who tried to take our land away, declared that we would never be able to raise the funds needed for a new campus. They said we would fail spectacularly. But they were up against an adversary like no other: moms and dads of disabled children.

As had happened throughout my life, if I was on the side of right and good and someone told me "no," I barreled on through. "No" was simply not an option.

I'll show them. We WILL raise the money and build this campus. And that's what we did!

The celebration took place on December 20th.

We hosted a small yet glamorous holiday reception to thank our amazing donors for their generous contributions. We had festive decor, libations, canapés, fantastic cookies created by local chefs and hot toddies.

High school students were recruited to light the 300 trees we borrowed from a local nursery; local design companies decorated the campus, a few hotels kicked in the garland décor, and the Stagehands Union set up the lights and sound so we could have a party with zero cost.

It quickly became evident that our guests, who came bundled up in fine furs and the spirit of the occasion, were enthralled by our campus that magically glittered with the accoutrements of the season.

After a successful reception, I sat on a bale of straw, tired and happy, realizing just how much people in the Las Vegas desert wanted a respite from the glitz and glamor of the Strip.

They longed to experience a more traditional holiday. They were struck by the beauty of the festive lights clinging to the small pine trees we had strategically placed.

Every attendee experienced a nostalgic homesickness brought on by our little magical forest that reminded them of home, family, and faraway places, and they asked if the lights and decorations could remain in place through Christmas.

Why not continue this experience for a few more days? Would people come away from the Strip to enjoy our little decorated corner of the world? We might even raise a few dollars! Could I create new holiday memories in a forest tucked away in an urban desert? I might be onto something big.

I jumped up from my straw bale and called my mom.

"Can you make a bunch of cookies tomorrow? A lot? I will make hot chocolate and sell them too. I am going to send a press release out overnight and see if people will come. If not, what do we have to lose? The cookies will get eaten!"

Then I called my brother, Terry, and his wife, Irene, who were visiting from England for the holidays, and asked them to give up their Christmas.

The next night, wrapped in winter garb, I hunkered down on my straw bale and waited to see what would happen.

Hordes of people showed up. The word had gone out across the valley. Local on-air personalities conducted live weather reports from our forest in the desert. Sometime that night, I named the project the Magical Forest.

A reporter on the eleven o'clock news announced, "There is this really cool walk-through holiday display, just west of the Strip in this unassuming neighborhood. We will be there tomorrow for a live broadcast." That's when I found out that an early morning broadcast meant the crew would be there at 5 a.m. and the lights were expected to be on.

The next few days were a blur. I dragged a small wishing well out from a closet, dusted it off, and placed it by my straw bale. We ran out after selling hundreds of hot chocolates and cookies. In one night, we raised a thousand dollars. Each night the donations from this impromptu fundraiser increased, and in a few days many more thousands were raised.

Zowie! An annual fundraiser was born that eventually grossed over $2 million each year with less than 15 percent expense. The Magical Forest sustained Opportunity Village for many years.

And so it was that several years into the Magical Forest event, on a cold December night, Debbie, my Canadian sister-in-law and friend, who traveled down from Canada each year to assist with the seasonal volunteer recruitment, was sitting in the boardroom at Opportunity Village finishing up her report on the volunteer activities, while the volunteers, outside in the bitter cold, closed down the ride booths and buttoned up the Magical Forest for the night.

Running a fifty-night fundraising marathon was no easy task. It required the recruitment of one hundred nightly volunteers, and I was grateful to Debbie and the wonderful staff and volunteers who toiled away each season with amazing dedication and love for both the event and the mission.

Lenny and Dave were two such volunteers. As members of the venerable Stagehands Union, these men could have made a ton of money on the Strip; instead they chose to make the world a better place, dedicating November and December to the service of their fellow citizens with special needs at great personal sacrifice.

After spending the last hour before the Magical Forest closed completing a proposal that had to go out in mid-December, I decided to go to the kitchen and bring back some treats that would warm the hearts and tummies of Debbie and my stagehand friends.

Growing up poor, I tended to be quite frugal, so instead of turning on the industrial lights in the huge training kitchen, I stumbled around the counters feeling my way in the dark to the walk-in refrigerator and freezer. I knew that when the doors opened, the light would automatically come on.

A veritable feast was waiting for me and my hard-working helpers. There was a yummy cake, alongside a plethora of cooked food, including BBQ sandwiches, cookies, and all kinds of drinks. I stepped into the walk-in fridge, and as I reached for the cake, the door slammed shut behind me, plunging me into utter darkness. *Oh boy. . .Now what?*

I was inside a large walk-in refrigerator at 10 p.m., and no one knew I was there. Fumbling in the dark, groping for a light switch, I felt my heart beating out of my chest as I realized there was no light.

Of course, who would be inside a refrigerator in need of a light?

I could hear the fan whirring, pushing colder air through the walk-in. Disoriented, I tripped on a case of beverages and fell into the wall. I was soon turned around and in full panic mode. I could not fathom how to get out. At some point, I recall feeling the outline of the door and realizing there was no handle to turn. Still I pushed as hard as I could to no avail.

After many minutes, I was as scared as I have ever been in my life. Tomorrow's headline flashed before my eyes.

"Noted fundraiser missing, last seen leaving her volunteers behind and heading out of her office in a quest for a bite to eat. Anyone having information call. . ." and then the next day's headline: *"Linda Smith found frozen in cooler."*

Please, God. . .Get me out of here.

It was glacially cold, and it felt as though I had been in this wretched refrigerator for an hour. I was literally freezing. Stumbling on a few crates, I considered stacking them and climbing on top in an attempt to reach up and still the fan. Another headline flashed in front of me:

"Woman electrocuted, bled to death, and frozen while inside a refrigerator after stupidly placing her hand inside an electric fan."

Staggering around in the confined space, my entire life flashed before me.

Please, God, don't end it here. Let me die doing something noble, courageous, not freezing to death because of a sweet tooth.

Desperate, I shouted, but I knew no one was within earshot to hear my muffled cries. It was Friday night, and no one would need the refrigerator till the following Monday. I could see it now. Sweet people with disabilities would be confronted by a frozen Linda when they opened the door.

I needed to do something soon or else I would die in here.

How long did it take to die in subzero temperatures?

Terrified, I shivered uncontrollably.

Okay, Linda, think. . . Rub your hands together, and feel around for something you can use as a possible hammer.

For what purpose, I had no idea, but at least I was mobile once more.

I traced the wall, hands stretched out, slowly groping my way around the small space, and then a rush of relief.

A door handle! How could that be? Is this a different door?

Elated, I turned the handle and the lights blazed on, and even colder air blew into my chamber. I was so relieved to see this new source of light that I almost leapt into this frigid space until it quickly dawned on me that this was the freezer. I jumped back into the refrigerator and let the freezer door slam shut, nearly fainting from shock and horror.

Oh, my God. . .What now? What would become of my boys? How would they go on without me? What a stupid and horrible way to die. If I were to freeze to death, couldn't it be doing something that was more honorable, like conquering Mount Everest?

I felt the panic well up. My heart raced faster, and my breathing became shallower.

Was I dying?

I felt the urge to give up, sit down and wait to die. Salty tears ran down my freezing cheeks.

Really God, is this it? Is this what you want for me?

I hated when I felt sorry for myself. It was pathetic.

And then I had a revelation. The light from the freezer would at least illuminate my predicament. Better to die with lights on than in the pitch black darkness.

With gritted teeth, I cautiously opened the freezer door again, allowing colder air to once more enter my tomb. The freezer light lit the way and in doing so oriented me to the cursed door I had originally entered. I could see the fan, the racks, the food. . . the path to the entry door with no handle that wouldn't open from the inside. In desperation, I let go of the freezer door and, enveloped in utter blackness once more, I ran at the refrigerator door like a linebacker, and it popped open!

It was a full week before I admitted my stupidity to anyone, and the only reason I did was when it occurred to me that this predicament could have happened to one of our disabled workers (probably not, as they would have been smart enough to prop the door open). A light and a handle were soon installed, and emergency training was promptly provided.

CHAPTER FORTY-SIX

AMNESTY

At last, a light at the end of the tunnel.

Since Christopher's birth, we had traveled across the country raising money and awareness for people with intellectual disabilities.

When Chris turned ten, we received an invitation to meet President Reagan at the White House. We were scheduled to go to Washington, D.C. on April 2, 1981.

We met Oklahoma Senator Finus Smith during one of Glenn's many engagements in that state. Upon hearing of our attempts to get Chris legalized, Senator Finus Smith championed our cause by introducing the "Christopher Smith Bill," which when approved did away with requiring medical intervention for anyone with a medical condition who wanted to immigrate to the U.S. After all Chris was not sick; he had a condition called Down syndrome,

Now we were to meet the President of the United States, and he would become our champion too.

Our family was credited with raising millions of dollars for disability causes, and the Arc, better known as The Association for Retarded Citizens, asked us to represent all American families with special needs kids and talk about discrimination. It was deemed the perfect opportunity to receive a presidential pardon for Chris and legalize him post-haste. We couldn't have been more proud.

As the presidential visit grew near, you could have picked our family off the ceiling. We tentatively went public with Chris' illegal status, and close friends called in their congratulations. We would travel with our two boys in Wayne's private plane to Washington, D.C.

Wayne was not only our friend and Jason's godfather, he had also just been named Honorary Chairman of the Arc with Glenn as the co-chair. We were on our way to make history with the leader of the free world in our corner.

On March 30, 1981, just two days shy of the momentous visit, President Ronald Reagan was shot in the chest by a deranged drifter named John Hinckley, Jr.

Needless to say, we did not go to Washington.

While I toiled away building Opportunity Village, a place my son would not be able to go to if he didn't gain legal status in the U.S., I kept my eye on the immigration laws and stayed in touch with people across the country who were trying to change the archaic laws pertaining to the admissibility of persons with disabilities into the country.

On November 6, 1986, the Immigration Reform and Control Act was signed into law by President Reagan. This law was designed to deal with illegal immigrants who entered the United States prior to January of 1982. If they could prove they had resided in the U.S. continuously and had paid taxes or were willing to pay a fine and any back taxes owed, they and their families would be welcomed as new citizens.

At last there was a light at the end of the tunnel.

The Immigration and Naturalization Service estimated about four million illegal immigrants would apply for legal status through the Act, with roughly half of them eligible for eventual citizenship. The odds were in our favor. Christopher was going to be one of the two million new U.S. citizens.

After many expensive conversations with the only immigration attorney worth his salt in Las Vegas, who assured us that the Amnesty Act was not designed to split up families, we applied to amnesty. We were the perfect candidates. We paid our taxes. We were legal residents of the U.S. We respected the laws of our adopted country and had raised tens of millions of dollars for people with disabilities and for many other causes. Glenn regularly appeared on national telethons for different charities, and we volunteered across the country when called upon. We did not associate with known felons or undesirables (except our son).

We couldn't be denied. Could we?

After several months of nervous waiting, the day for our interview came. We dressed respectfully for the occasion, brought our attorney as back-up, and rolled the dice. We stood out in the crowd as we waited patiently and optimistically, as most of the amnesty applicants were of Hispanic descent.

When the time came to talk with the interviewer, we followed our attorney's advice and divulged the truth about Christopher's present status and our quest for citizenship for him for the past sixteen years. We told how we lost his vice-presidential sponsor, resorting to breaking the law and keeping him in the country illegally. The interviewer understood. This was fabulous.

Together we filled out copious amounts of paperwork that would be sent on to Washington, D.C., where our fate would be determined. Several more months went by as we watched the amnesty program take effect on live television: A million or more people were legalized, granted residency, and reunited with their families. Our wait would soon be over, and we would be able to breathe freely.

Anticipating that Christopher would soon be a full-fledged American, we began to open up and tell people outside of our close circle of his present status in the U.S. People were shocked to hear that Chris was illegal, but they understood our need for confidentiality all these years. No one wanted to see us deported. We had become members of a tight community, a fundraising machine for disability causes, and had amassed powerful and influential friends. It was simply a matter of time before Chris became legal, and we planned to have a huge celebration. It would be a blow-out party, and we would promote it and make national news and people would be outraged once they became aware of the discrimination our family had experienced.

The day of reckoning finally arrived. We would probably have to pay a fine, but that would be the worst of it. We were ready. What we were not ready for was outright rejection.

Sitting in front of a composed government worker once more, we were shocked when we heard that our application had been denied. The interviewer said he was sorry, but there was nothing he could do. Shrugging his shoulders, he read the decision. Chris fell into "a certain exclusionary category." We should take him out of the country and apply for residency from the Canadian side of the border.

I don't remember much else that was said during the interview. Christopher sat alongside us, smiling, unaware and thankfully not understanding that he was still classified as undesirable. My little guy had inspired a movement of love and support for the disabled in Las Vegas, but he wasn't worthy of residency in the United States. I could not believe what I was hearing. We were stunned when we left the office.

Amnesty

I was so convinced he would be accepted. After all this time spent fighting the system, filling out mountains of paperwork and sitting for hours in immigration offices waiting our turn, Chris was still considered an undesirable alien. To soften the blow, we were told his classification had been downgraded. He was no longer the second most undesirable class; he was now sixth in line behind Communists and people with infectious diseases, but before anarchists and subversives.

In short, Chris would not gain legal status.

Through Christopher's eyes, I mostly saw goodness and kindness in people, a perspective that was common in families like mine. Unfortunately, that outlook wasn't enough to overcome the ongoing fight to gain legal status for our son.

Statistics cite that eighty percent of marriages failed with the addition of a disabled child. Added to that was the complications of being married to a very popular traveling musician, an entertainer's wife in Las Vegas, and the major distractions of my own forays into disability advocacy.

My quest to make people see the intrinsic value of disabled people, raise needed funds, and bring awareness to the cause was all encompassing. I became a fundraising machine immersed in advocacy and community relations. I wasn't proud that I had pressed all our friends into becoming donors, our family members were full-time volunteers, our home was the fundraising headquarters, and Glenn was the main attraction for the annual Glenn Smith Concert of Love.

Inevitably the pressure of feeling responsible for Chris' needs, as well as all Southern Nevadans with disabilities put a strain on every relationship I had, including my marriage to Glenn. Not even the birth of our second son, Jason, a much-loved addition to the family, was enough to save us. We parted when Chris was fourteen and Jason was seven.

It was a relief when Glenn moved out of our home and into a bachelor pad. We had been living separate lives. I was no longer an entertainer, and the only common ground we now had were the children. At the time, Glenn was dating the lead dancer in his own show on the Las Vegas strip. He confided in me that he told her I wouldn't divorce him as a convenient way to keep the relationship untangled, and if I didn't mind, he would use this line as an excuse in all his relationships. He was quite clear that he would never marry again, or have more children.

I said, "Sure thing, Glenn." I would help him like I helped everyone.

Our separation was amicable, though I envied his freedom. He was a busy entertainer who worked nights, while I was a mom to two children, one with multiple disabilities, as well as a full-time breadwinner with a ton of vulnerable people depending on me.

I would go to work each day welcomed by a chorus of sweet voices. "Hi, Linda, how are you? You look nice; have you lost weight? Want some of my lunch? You look like Tina Turner! Can I have a paper clip?" These were the most optimistic, vulnerable people in the world, and I was worried about letting them down. Who was I, anyway? What qualifications did I have? I had no real training for this important job, but these trusting people had placed all their eggs in my basket, and they were depending on me.

I had always enjoyed Glenn's celebrity status to get what I needed; he was my ace in the hole. Now that I was on my own, it was important to remain friends. With the responsibility of a larger-than-life job, a big house, my mom, our dog, Christopher and Jason, life at times felt like a house of cards.

Although he wasn't perfect, it must be said that Glenn never shirked his responsibilities toward our boys who he loved, so we chugged along as best we could with me shouldering the everyday care. My disabled boy needed a lifetime of care from at least one parent, and that was me.

My job was my future; I no longer had a future with Glenn. In the end, I went quietly into the night. Few people knew we had separated. In that way, we could continue to present this image of the ideal couple, parents of a disabled child who were raising money together for a great cause.

And then one day even my faux marriage to Glenn was taken away. I was at the office, scrambling to unearth every dollar in town, when a process server arrived at our door and announced himself, he was serving me with divorce papers. Glenn had suddenly decided to marry his young bass player and have more children.

We had gone through so much together and managed to remain cordial throughout the separation process. I had strad-dled the line that so many broken marriages do—whether to remain friends or become enemies. I had chosen to take the high road, and this approach by Glenn was a low blow.

The serving of the divorce papers was the beginning of the end for the fundraising machine that was Glenn and Linda, with the annual Concert of Love ending when Glenn's new family took precedence.

CHAPTER \ FORTY-SEVEN

A SNOWSTORM IN WASHINGTON

"I am the proud mother of an illegal alien."

I was very angry as I walked out of the immigration building holding a rejection slip that said our son wasn't worthy of being an American. He would soon turn eighteen, and once he reached that age, he would never be eligible to legally live in the U.S. due to the mandatory requirements of citizenship.

I didn't give a damn about the outcome of exposing Christopher's status anymore. I was outraged that our family was not welcome. If this country didn't want us, we would leave. But we wouldn't go without a long, expensive fight that we would take to the Supreme Court if necessary.

What a loss for the country! Glenn and I had raised hundreds of millions of dollars through benefit concerts and telethons and through my work at Opportunity Village.

Chris' birth brought awareness to the plight of the disabled through the efforts of his family and friends. I was sick and tired of my son not being considered worthy. We would not go quietly into the night. We would shout from the highest mountain.

I ordered T-shirts that said, "I am the proud mother of an illegal alien." Christopher's shirt said, "I am an alien."

Once Chris turned eighteen he would be an adult and would have to meet certain requirements to be apply for citizenship.

1) He had to have lived as a legal immigrant in the U.S. for a specific period of time. *One black mark.*

2) He had to have good moral character and not be convicted of certain crimes. *One mark in his favor.*

3) He had to speak, read, and write in English. *Oops, not our boy, unless "shit," "damn," and "NO" constituted knowledge of the English language.*

4) He had to know the basics of U.S. history, government, and civics. *Most definitely a no.*

5) And last, he must understand and have an attachment to the U.S. Constitution. *We were toast.*

He needed to be legal now, before he turned eighteen.

Milestones in my life seemed to happen during snowstorms. On October 16, 1987, I flew from Las Vegas to Washington, D.C. to attend a national disability conference (for the Arc, The Association for Retarded Citizens). I was going to be a presenter at this gathering of 2,000 disability professionals. By this time, I was a respected and sought-after fundraiser and would lead a session on philanthropic giving the next morning.

Unfortunately, my flight was delayed due to bad weather. By the time my plane landed, I missed the opening plenary and several sessions pertinent to my presentation the following day

At best, I would arrive in the middle of the opening night dinner. I wondered if I should skip the dinner, get a good night's sleep, and chalk it up as part of the travails of travel, or should I at least make an appearance? Over the years, The Arc leadership had done everything they could to get Chris legal status, and though we hadn't succeeded, I owed them a lot for trying.

After ten hours of flight delays and changes, I finally checked into the conference hotel. Exhausted from traveling, the long lines at baggage claim, and longer taxi lines, I turned on the TV while I hurriedly dumped the contents of my suitcase onto the bed, and saw a breaking news report that an eighteen-month-old baby named Jessica had fallen into a well on her family's farm in Midland, Texas.

Hundreds of people were attempting to extricate this little girl from the well, and millions of viewers were transfixed by the brave little toddler who was humming tunes deep down in the ground. The news was riveting as CNN, then a fledgling station, broadcast round-the-clock coverage.

I wanted to change into my nightgown, order room service, work on my speech for tomorrow, and watch this compelling story rather than get dressed up and go downstairs to a rubber chicken dinner for two thousand bored guests that was probably already half over.

Muttering to myself, I griped about the lateness of the hour, the prospect of walking into a commodious banquet room alone, and the pros and cons of foregoing the occasion.

C'mon, Linda. . . You flew all the way here to go to the conference. Are you really going to stay in your room tonight?

This is something I do often. I am the most indecisive person I know. *Should I do this? Or should I do that?* I knew for certain that I wouldn't be missed. I didn't have guests at a table waiting for me.

I checked the room service menu. *The 'carte du jour' featured a nice gumbo and a recommended wine choice, and maybe a small dish of ice cream for dessert. That sounded yummy.*

If I was going to go, I would have to steam my dress in the shower. Continuing the conversation in my head, I obsessed about the responsibility of this trip to D.C., the late hour, the fact that after taking a quick shower, I would have to put my make-up back on, heat up the curling iron, and find the deodorant, not to mention poor Baby Jessica. Guilt and indecisiveness plagued my life.

In the end, duty called. I needed to go to this dinner no matter how late the hour. I said a prayer for Baby Jessica, who was still in the well unbelievably humming songs, while drills hammered away on a mission to free her. Some guy with no shoulders had volunteered to go down the narrow shaft and pluck her out, and new, improved pneumatic drills arrived on the scene, while I grudgingly made my way to the conference center.

As expected, the cavernous hotel conference center was a beehive of activity. Two thousand souls from across the country were engaged in eating, talking, and comparing stories. The noisy cacophony of conversations drowned out the large orchestra on stage that was playing dreadful background music which was being piped through a poor sound system.

The room was brightly lit and stuffy, with the disgusting smell of fish permeating the air. The floral arrangements on the tables were wilted and put together in an unattractive way that only a national nonprofit organization with no budget could manage. It was obvious that I had made a bad choice in coming and was in for a boring evening.

As I looked around I saw that there were no seats and the harried wait staff was too busy clearing the salad plates and bringing out both the entrée and the dessert at once, which was certain to be cheesecake, which I loathed, to help me.

I made my way between tables searching for a friendly face, or more importantly, an empty seat, only to realize it was a futile endeavor. I circled the room looking in every direction hoping to catch the eye of a kind soul who would indicate an available seat, but all the guests were engrossed in conversation and not interested in this latecomer.

Admittedly I felt a tad relieved as I looked for the closest exit. *It's not my fault. I tried, but there were simply no seats to be found, and the staff was too busy to help me.*

I turned to go, thoughts of Baby Jessica and room service gumbo already on my mind. Then from out of the blue, a shout came from across the room.

"Over here! Do you need a seat? There is one here!"

Now I had no excuse. I must feign appreciation. Once I was settled and my order was taken—as anticipated, *"chicken or fish"* and *"cheesecake for dessert?"*—I conjured up a smile.

Attempting to raise my voice above the din, I shouted to the person to my left, "Hi, I'm Linda. I'm sorry I'm late. My flight was delayed. I almost didn't make it. Boy, this room is packed. Thanks for the seat. Did you hear about Baby Jessica who is trapped in a well in Texas?"

I was certain that my tablemates, who had already spent ninety minutes standing in line at the bar to purchase an expensive glass of cheap wine, and trying to avoid being crushed when the doors opened and everyone rushed to secure a table preferably near an exit so they could escape unnoticed before the night was over, weren't interested in listening to me.

Then the large, vociferous woman, who had enthusiastically invited me over, continued her impassioned welcome, shouting a greeting across the table. It turned out she was from Reno, Nevada.

*I thought it an interesting coincidence that w*ith two thousand people in the room, I was at a table with a fellow Nevadan.

She said she was there representing a small disability organization called the Washoe Arc, and asked where I was from.

"I'm Linda Smith from "Las Vegas," I shouted. "My son, Christopher has Down syndrome. . .I am a presenter tomorrow. It's a fundraising session. . .You should come."

The woman shouted back, "I know you. I'm planning on going to your session. I have followed your story over the years. You have a Canadian son that you have been trying to get legal status for in the U.S...right? How is it going?"

With that, all heads turned in my direction.

Cool, I would share with this group my jaw-dropping story about our ongoing fight to get Christopher legal in the U.S. If nothing else, it would make the dinner go by faster. If only it wasn't so freaking loud in here.

My head was pounding from the smoke, the fish, and the noise. But after downing a glass of wine in one big gulp, I went for the shock factor and shouted back, "It's not going well. Christopher is approaching eighteen and still illegal. He is still subject to deportation."

Several tables surrounding us went silent, and heads turned in our direction, straining to hear.

Good, a larger audience.

"If I don't get him legal soon, he will be disqualified forever." And then in defiance, I shouted, "IT'S CRAZY. I AM HARBORING AN ILLEGAL ALIEN IN MY HOME, AND IT'S MY OWN SON. I DON'T CARE ANYMORE. LET THEM TRY TO DEPORT ME. I WON'T GO DOWN WITHOUT A FIGHT!"

I had become emboldened, bolstered by crisscrossing the country and helping organizations and families raise millions of dollars and tons of awareness for the disabled. In doing so, I had met a lot of influential people, and at this point, I truly didn't give a hoot if immigration came after me. I would call in my markers and take my fight all the way to the president if necessary. I also knew that beneath my bravado was fear.

Through this exchange, the well-dressed couple sitting immediately to my right leaned forward, appearing very interested in the conversation. The gentleman had politely stood and pulled out my chair when I arrived at their table, and the woman he was with was an attractive Asian woman with a welcoming smile.

At the end of my outburst, I reached for the wine bottle, intent on swallowing another full glass before heading out the door when the gentleman softly asked if I would enlighten him further. He was captivated and urged me to tell him EVERYTHING.

And so I did.

I spent the next fifteen minutes gulping wine and indignantly laying out the past seventeen-and-a-half-year journey. His wife sat quietly listening as best she could and occasionally nodded her head. It turned out she spoke very little English. After quizzing me on several points, he introduced himself and handed me his card.

His name was Bob Anderson, and he was the Head of U.S.A. Immigration and Naturalization!

On this fortuitous day in Washington, D.C., my plane was late, Baby Jessica was stuck in a well, and in a room jam packed with two thousand strangers, I happened to sit next to the one person who could help me. He could also hurt me and report us to the INS; but instead, he took our family's information and put it on the top of his pile, addressing Chris' case the very next working day.

This kind man had taken a Chinese citizen as his wife, and in doing so, he had adopted her disabled daughter and fought his own battle to get her legal in the U.S. This man, who could have had me arrested, instead became our champion. He retrieved our files and years of paperwork, moved our case to the top of the pile, and fixed a seventeen-and-a-half-year problem, paving the way for Christopher to become a legal resident of the United States.

CHAPTER FORTY-EIGHT

VICTORY AT LAST

His birth provided me with a noble goal.

Christopher's birth formed my future. He gave my life meaning and purpose. He turned his self-absorbed, entertainer
mom into a community activist, an advocate of the disabled,
and a take-no-prisoners fundraising icon.

He changed his little brother's life too, as Jason dove into
disability causes and became an innovative and respected
fundraising leader himself.

Jason is an interesting mix of disability advocate and fundraiser like his mom and a talented musician and singer like
his dad. Taking the stage at the annual Concert of Love at
the age of three, with an adoring Christopher watching, he
melted hearts and became a valuable member of the Smith
fundraising machine, appearing in every Concert of Love until
the last one.

The Concert of Love began when Chris was born, and it became the core of our lives, a metaphor for life with Christopher. A clarion call went out to show-business friends, and they came together *en masse*. They heard that a special child was born to a member of their special club, this "club" a society, a union, an alliance of people who lived to entertain and inspire minds and touch hearts with spectacles of joy and happiness through their craft. They heard that a child needed help, and they responded to that call.

The first Concert of Love took place in Ontario, Canada. That's when my education as a disability activist started. I was a quick study because I had to be. I had no degree. I was a high-school dropout. All I had were street smarts and an understanding of the simple premise that people give because they are asked. That being told "no" just gets you closer to a "yes." That it felt good to give and know you were making a difference. That every dollar counted, no matter the denomination.

I learned to say thank you for every gift, not once, not twice, but ten times or more. To practice "eyes and ears before mouth." To treat every donor not as a donor, but as a friend. I would tell them how their money would be used and who would benefit, and how their support would make an enormous difference in so many lives.

As a mom, I wanted to dive into something more meaningful and was pleasantly surprised when I was asked to be OV's first fundraiser.

I conducted a capital campaign in my first year on the job, raising a million dollars for a resource center adjacent to the thrift store where I volunteered whenever I was in Las Vegas.

I then headed up five subsequent campaigns and built state-of-the-art campuses throughout the valley.

I created signature events like the Meatball Festival, the Concert of Love, the Turkey Trot, Miss Kitty's Jeans to Jewels, the BBQ at the Bitterroot Ranch, Camelot, the Magical Forest, and the Las Vegas Great Santa Run.

Victory at last

I started the first endowments through payroll donations named for my boy, The Christopher Smith Recreation Fund.

As a fundraising professional, I shared my knowledge, admonishing fundraisers who saw a donor as an entity that should be segmented into categories of giving. A donor is a human being with the same needs, wants, and desires to help as the next guy. He is not a target. Everyone can give, and everyone should be given the opportunity to contribute to society.

I taught by example, approaching the most unlikely candidates: the carpenter, the plumber, the electrician, the union worker, the bartender, the cocktail server, and the prison system. Those are the people who fly below the radar of every nonprofit leader. It's with that crowd that I honed my solicitation skills. They became my base—loyal donors who hung in there, year after year after year. They are the people to whom I owe much of my fundraising success.

As I became adept at this unplanned career, I came to realize that I was not asking, but instead I was giving: giving people an opportunity to be part of something magical, to be part of a society intent on making the world a better place. When used for the greater good, for those in need, philanthropy represented the heart and soul of humanity.

The sold-out concerts launched a journey and became an initiative that transported a mother and her child from the depths of sadness onto a stage of unimaginable significance. All I did was ask, and a whole bunch of people followed.

Early into the "Education of Linda," I adopted the mantra "'No' is not an option." I simply could not take "no" for an answer. "No" was a part of my story from my earliest days as a child. "No" never meant defeat. Instead it was a chance to go back with a different approach. "No" simply meant "not now," or "not this project," or even "not you," but those no's spurred me on. An easy "yes" meant I had not asked for enough. Give me a "no" before an easy "yes," any day.

I knocked on every door and wouldn't leave without something, no matter the perceived value. At times, that something was simply an open door to return. That was a win.

I spoke to a group of professionals at a luncheon one day, and in the middle of my speech, I was interrupted by a member of the audience who shared her experience of a time when I called her boss and asked for a contribution. In asking this man how she should handle my request, he said, "Give her what she wants or she will never give up." That brought plenty of laughter from the crowd, but it was true.

I have been called indefatigable and unrelenting in my quest to not just raise funds and awareness for the disabled, but to bring humanity to Las Vegas. Some perceived Las Vegas as an inhospitable town of megalomaniacal tycoons, mobsters, and entertainers, who made their way to our city intent on fame and fortune, and when the stars didn't align, settled for being showgirls, dealers, and bartenders.

That has not been my experience. Every Concert of Love brought wonderful, giving, generous people from every station of life into my circle. The Concerts of Love that were performed in Canada, New York, and for twenty-five years in Las Vegas, changed the way thousands of people viewed disability. Additionally, the concerts transformed philanthropy in Las Vegas by engaging the hearts and minds of our city's hardscrabble citizens, who joined a movement and became better citizens because of it.

These events altered the way tough-minded casino moguls viewed philanthropy. I wasn't there with my hand held out as if I were a beggar. I was a mom on a mission to give my son's life meaning. As a novice in the art of fundraising and show production, I felt the strong need to gather talented people and share my vision with them. And I succeeded spectacularly.

Victory at last

Perhaps there is something to say for naiveté, for believing in a dream and inspiring others to make that dream their own. In my quest to raise money for the cause of disability, I met the most talented, kind, and generous people, thanks to my son.

To say one baby sent an entire city on an unexpected journey would underestimate the impact of Christopher's life. My son is a change maker. With his mom as his champion, he caused a revolution, a big societal change to happen. His birth provided me with a noble goal: I would change the world. At the very least, I would mold my adopted city into a place I could be proud to call home.

We raised millions of dollars and built a small organization called Opportunity Village into a world-class program and campus, yet our son could not go there. He was illegal right up until fate smiled on us, and I sat down next to a man on his own mission to help the disabled.

On a Sunday afternoon on February 14, 1988—Valentine's Day—just two months and one day short of Chris' eighteenth birthday, my boy finally stepped onto the stage at the Concert of Love in the Las Vegas Hilton Hotel's main showroom, where Elvis Presley, Barbra Streisand, and Liberace, had performed, and in front of 1,200 guests and hundreds of loyal friends, including Wayne Newton, the entire cast of the *Follies Bergere*, Senator Harry Reid, Governor Richard Bryan, and the Honorable Judge Lloyd D. George presiding, Christopher stood during his naturalization ceremony and was handed an American flag that had flown over the Capital.

My beautiful, brave son, Christopher, was finally a legal resident of the United States of America.

Chris receiving the American Flag on stage at the Hilton Hotel with his dad and brother, Jason, alongside Jerry Tarkanian, Senator Richard Bryan, Senator Harry Reid, and Wayne Newton.

EPILOGUE

Giving birth to a multiply-disabled child changed the trajectory of my life and provided me with a sense of purpose and eventually an altruistic career. When the dark picture of Christopher's future and ours was presented, I resolved to become his advocate and throw my lot into the special needs world. It wasn't easy, and there were many doubts and fears, hospital stays, and heartaches. This was not the life I pictured, but it became the life I lived.

Sure, there were regrets. He was, after all, the first child, the first grandchild, the first nephew in the family. But Christopher opened us all up to a special kind of love, and he is a much-loved member of our family, adored by his brother, his aunts and uncles, cousins and friends.

Even as we kept a round-the-clock vigil at the hospital in the early weeks of his life, it became apparent that Chris changed perceptions and lives. The medical teams soon realized that he was not a sad statistic; he was loved and valued, his life had meaning, and his life's work was yet to be done.

With Christopher eighteen, fully legal, and finally secure in his adopted country, he was eligible to take part in the programs at Opportunity Village. By then, I was Vice President of Philanthropy for an organization that had fast become a leader throughout the world in the field of disability services and philanthropic giving.

Against all odds—with a "take no prisoners/no is not an option" approach—and plenty of moxie, I helped build an organization like no other, a place that would be visited by sitting presidents, celebrities, and community leaders from across the continent. I prevailed on friends like Elvis, Wayne Newton, Celine Dion, Shania Twain, and Penn and Teller to help turn my ideas into much-touted and beloved signature events.

Together with my colleague and friend Ed Guthrie, we conceived of and built four state-of-the-art campuses and put fifty million dollars in the bank, with millions more in estate gifts still to come, thus helping to secure the organization's future. I raised half a billion dollars for Opportunity Village and millions more for charitable causes throughout the world.

In October 2016, after thirty-five years of non-stop fundraising, I left my beloved organization. I had accomplished more than I ever dreamed I could there.

I am now a fundraising consultant, a motivational speaker, an author, and a wife again. It would be twenty years before I found and married a wonderful man named John, who I met because of Christopher.

John was a Wyoming cowboy, rancher, entrepreneur, and a Las Vegas business leader; a man for all seasons with a heart of gold and a kindness that shone through at hello. My quest to make the world better for all people with disabilities brought me to his doorstep. I met John when I asked for the ongoing support of his company. He was the CEO of

Budweiser in Las Vegas, and at the ribbon cutting of OV's first campus that I raised the monies for, I noticed he was not part of the VIP tour. He had snuck out, trading the spotlight for some backroom communing with a group of our most profoundly disabled citizens. It was at that moment my heart began to soar, and I fell in love with my future husband.

The odds of a second marriage taking place when there was a disabled child in the equation were next to zero. But John loved and accepted my boys, and I am forever thankful to be married to this kind, beautiful man. He is my best friend, my biggest fan, and my rock.

My mom danced to the end and died at age ninety-two. Jean gave up on show business and now lives on the Vancouver Coast while Terry and his wife, Irene, who got married at sixteen, recently celebrated their 50th anniversary in England.

Jason, although an accomplished musician like his dad, followed his mom into the world of philanthropy and is making his own mark in the charitable sector. I am so proud of him. He is happily married to Krysti, a gifted and lovely girl, and they have given me a beautiful granddaughter named Lilyclaire.

Jason has established a legacy for his brother through the Christopher Smith Foundation, a charitable advocacy organization that will fight for the rights of kids like our Christopher.

Christopher has defied the doctors' predictions and thrived. He is loved by his wonderful friends and caregivers Sonny and Raquel. There are not enough words to express my gratitude to them. At Opportunity Village, he became a "Document Destruction Specialist" aka a paper shredder. Chris doesn't understand the value of the paycheck he receives every two weeks—in fact he loves to shred it after he waves it proudly in the air alongside his buddies. His life has value, just as all our lives do. That is only part of what I have learned by being Christopher's mom. He changed our lives and gave my life meaning.

I have come a long way from that sad little English girl and am now living an unimagined life. When handed a basket of lemons, I chose to make the best lemonade I could, and I am thankful for all the lessons along the way. It's been my privilege to be Christopher's mom and to have experienced his innocence and unconditional love.

Like so many other mothers, I look back and see how my journey with my special boy has enriched me in ways I would never have believed, ways that will be forever cherished. I am eternally grateful for a life I would have initially done anything to avoid.

Chris is beautiful, otherworldly, unique, and oh so very precious. He possesses an infinite capacity to love freely and wholeheartedly, without inhibition.

This is love, true love, in its purest form, and I can't imagine a life without him in it. I took an unforeseen detour, and it became the most unexpected, glorious journey. I am so glad to have taken it.

"This Child"

A song for Christopher
by Glenn Smith.

This child like your child
Was conceived like any other
By a father and mother in love

This child like your child
Came into this life
By a husband and a wife
Who had love to give
To a new human being

Epilogue

This child has to learn,
Has to live, has to love
He must be the best that he can be

This child must be free
Must have equality
After all this child's one of us
Give this child a hand
Let's do all we can
Don't you think we must?
Because after all this child's one of us

ACKNOWLEDGMENTS

I've always known I had a unique story to tell, which I shared often in my job as a communicator in the nonprofit world; but I never imagined I would pen a memoir.

They say you are rich if you have one true friend. Well, I have an abundance of riches, and l am eternally grateful to every person who has shown me what true friendship means.

My friend Bobby Bigelow was the first to kick me into gear with his daily words of encouragement. "Have you started? How many words today? Put the damn vacuum cleaner away and get to work!" His calls were what I needed to get me out of my funk after I left a 35-year career that I loved and found myself adrift without a compass. But that's another book.

My dearest friend Carol Troesh is central in my recent successes as a new author, consultant, motivational speaker, and world traveler. Carol and her sweet sister Gail encouraged me every step of the way and opened my eyes to the possibilities. I owe a huge debt of gratitude to these fabulous women.

Longtime friends, identical twins Jackie Singer and Mollie Miller, cheered me on daily and brought their equally talented twin daughters, also named Jackie and Mollie, on my journey. I am indebted to them for the tons of hours spent de-wonking the manuscript, formatting, designing, explaining tweets and blogs, recommending web and social media platforms and bringing me fabulous homemade desserts. I am indebted to this fab foursome, each a talented musician, vocalist and entrepreneur.

Thank you to my wonderful editor, Trai Cartwright, who spurred me on, made me believe in my abilities, and saw more books in me.

Thank you to my new pal, Larry Bennett at Nord Compo, who made the right introductions at the right time.

Thank you to my beta reader friends, too many to mention who bravely slogged through the first 100,000 unedited words. Their kindness means the world to me.

To celebrity scribe, Marsala Rypka, who provided a safe place for me to recall those early childhood memories that I had long buried when she interviewed me for a lengthy magazine article. Listening to my story, she urged me to write this book. Marsala is more than a dream interviewer, an illuminator of persons of great fame, and legendary celebrity writer in Las Vegas, she is a friend. Wanting my book to be the best it could possibly be, she graciously edited, rearranged, and polished the words of this first time author's final manuscript into the shiny tome that it now is. She did this with a kindness and grace that she is known for. Thank you my friend.

Most important is family. My fabulous husband, John is always patient, loving, and my biggest fan and confidant.

Through it all there was my son, Jason, whose enthusiasm and reassurances spurred me forward. He reminded me of forgotten details and helped bring perception and value to stories that I might not have told. His fierce and protective heart helped me forget the bad spaces; his optimism and intelligence won the day and created chapters. Jason and his beautiful wife, Krysti, gave birth to my precious grandbaby Lilyclaire midway through the writing, thus providing perspective and color that was woven into the chapters about motherhood.

And then there is Christopher. My angel son, the inspiration for all that I do. His love and belief in his mom is

Acknowledgments

unequivocal, pure, and simple. He will never read this book and won't know the impact his life has had on his family and on the world, but the first book off the press is most deservedly his.